# PEDAGOGIES OF PROXIMITY

## The Making of an Itinerant School

*Cristina D. Vintimilla and Veronica Pacini-Ketchabaw*

*Pedagogies of Proximity* presents an innovative response to the challenges of the pandemic by recounting the experience of an itinerant early childhood school in Cuenca, Ecuador, which operated in home gardens as an alternative to online learning.

Co-authored by leading scholars in early childhood education, Cristina D. Vintimilla and Veronica Pacini-Ketchabaw, this book examines how the pandemic paradoxically intensified neoliberal educational logics while also creating an opportunity to interrupt those very forces. Blending theory, research, and lived experiences, *Pedagogies of Proximity* presents a compelling argument for a holistic educational environment, responsiveness to the timeliness of educational events, and the value of pedagogical experimentation. Drawing from a diverse range of literature and cultural contexts, including Andean cosmology, the authors contextualize their work within local traditions and global educational discourse.

*Pedagogy of Proximities* is a timely and relevant text for educational scholars, graduate students, and educators. Vintimilla and Pacini-Ketchabaw allow us to truly ask the question of what is important in creating an educational experience, as well as how we might let the political and cultural dimensions of our world impact education.

CRISTINA D. VINTIMILLA is an associate professor of early childhood in the Faculty of Education at York University and a pedagogista.

VERONICA PACINI-KETCHABAW is a professor of early childhood education in the Faculty of Education and director of the Interdisciplinary Centre for Research in Curriculum at Western University.

# Pedagogies of Proximity

## *The Making of an Itinerant School*

CRISTINA D. VINTIMILLA AND
VERONICA PACINI-KETCHABAW

UNIVERSITY OF TORONTO PRESS
Toronto Buffalo London

Toronto Buffalo London
utppublishing.com
Printed in Canada

ISBN 978-1-4875-4959-6 (cloth) ISBN 978-1-4875-5877-2 (EPUB)
ISBN 978-1-4875-5239-8 (paper) ISBN 978-1-4875-5611-2 (PDF)

---

**Library and Archives Canada Cataloguing in Publication**

Title: Pedagogies of Proximity : the making of an itinerant school / Cristina D. Vintimilla and Veronica Pacini-Ketchabaw.
Names: Vintimilla, Cristina Delgado, author. | Pacini-Ketchabaw, Veronica, author
Description: Includes bibliographical references and index.
Identifiers: Canadiana (print) 20250217732 | Canadiana (ebook) 20250217805 | ISBN 9781487552398 (softcover) | ISBN 9781487549596 (hardcover) | ISBN 9781487558772 (EPUB) | ISBN 9781487556112 (PDF)
Subjects: LCSH: Culturally relevant pedagogy – Ecuador – Cuenca – Case studies. | LCSH: Culturally sustaining pedagogy – Ecuador – Cuenca – Case studies. | LCSH: School environment – Ecuador – Cuenca – Case studies. | LCSH: Alternative education – Ecuador – Cuenca – Case studies.
Classification: LCC LC1099.515.C85 V56 2025 | DDC 370.11/5 – dc23

---

Cover design: Kristjan Buckingham
Cover image: Illustrated by Clara Valeria León Gutiérrez

We wish to acknowledge the land on which the University of Toronto Press operates. This land is the traditional territory of the Wendat, the Anishnaabeg, the Haudenosaunee, the Métis, and the Mississaugas of the Credit First Nation.

This book has been published with the help of a grant from the Federation for the Humanities and Social Sciences, through the Awards to Scholarly Publications Program, using funds provided by the Social Sciences and Humanities Research Council of Canada.

University of Toronto Press acknowledges the financial support of the Government of Canada, the Canada Council for the Arts, and the Ontario Arts Council, an agency of the Government of Ontario, for its publishing activities.

Funded by the Government of Canada | Financé par le gouvernement du Canada | Canada

*To the children of Santana School: Children's City who refused a virtual education during the COVID-19 pandemic.*

*Una escuela que se gestiona a sí misma es una escuela que está leyendo continuamente las relaciones que la constituyen. Y esas relaciones son concretas y cotidianas. En el día a día, lo que nos hace pensar, lo que nos inquieta, lo que nos provoca malestar o alegría, lo que nos hace pregunta es el contacto con los otros. Por eso una escuela que se gestiona a sí misma no está pensando moralmente cuán cerca o lejos está el Estado, sino la relación con los otros con los que se encuentra todos los días.*

Silvia Duschatzky and Elina Aguirre

*A school that gestates itself is a school that is continually reading the relationships that constitute it. And those relationships are situated and quotidian. On a day-to-day basis, what makes us think, what worries us, what causes us discomfort or joy, what makes us question is the encounter with others. That is why a school that gestates itself is not morally thinking about how close or far the State is, but about the relationships with those whom it continuously encounters.*

Silvia Duschatzky and Elina Aguirre

# Contents

# Illustrations

# Acknowledgments

We are profoundly grateful to acknowledge that the creation of this book and the making of the itinerant school have been nothing short of a collaborative and collective endeavour. This experimental space stands as witness that our work is always contaminated by the inspiring conversations and exchanges we have had over many decades with our outstanding colleagues and friends in North and South America. Any omissions and errors are entirely our own.

There is no question that this book – and the itinerant school, in particular – embodies the shared and collective learnings from the teachers and pedagogical leaders at Experiencia Educativa Santana: La Ciudad de los Niñxs (Santana Children's City) Cuenca, Ecuador. We thank Estefania, Marieli, Valeria, Ximena, Andrea, Carolina, Cristina, Karina, Maria Cecilia, Goti, and Carolina for their dedication and everything they put into making the itinerant school, including at times when neoliberal forces made it very difficult to move on. This endeavour would not have been possible without the dedication of the larger Santana school community, whose different ways embraced and nurtured our vision for the itinerant school. To this end, we are indebted to the families who weaved with us and their children, embracing struggles along the way and creating the beautiful tapestry of the itinerant school. We could not have engaged in this educational experimentation without the unwavering support that Pablo Augusto Crespo continues to provide to our work through his thoughtful leadership. We are truly grateful. We would not have learned so much about creating an alternative educational space if Pablo had not invited us to think with Santana about our global circumstances and had he not responded to our invitation call with a resounding yes back in 2016.

The analyses expressed in this book are the sole responsibility of the authors and do not reflect the views of Santana. However, Santana respects and values the rigor of the research and the findings presented in this publication. Santana remains committed to maintaining a positive relationship and continued collaboration with the authors as it is Santana's view that this collaboration has enriched their pedagogical perspectives.

We express our sincere appreciation to Alex Berry and Alicja Frankowski for walking alongside us, the teachers, and the children during the making of the itinerant school. Their invaluable contributions to the book have significantly enriched it.

We extend our deepest appreciation to our colleagues and friends who contributed their time, expertise, and passion to this project, including Sara Sutherland, Bo Sun Kim, Kathleen Kummen, Walter Kohan, Sylvia Kind, and Tatiana Zhakarova Goodman. They reminded us that experimentation in education is still possible.

We are grateful for the opportunity to collaborate, in the Canadian component of this project, with our dear colleague Anne Phelan and for the multiple movements in thought that our conversations with her created.

We are grateful to Tatiana Zakharova Goodman for designing the exquisite itinerant school website. Tatiana's continuous support and companionship throughout the journey have been invaluable. Tatiana, Teresa Humprey, and Valeria Leon created the stunning speculative drawings that indicate the projecting potentiality of pedagogical documentation. These drawings are featured in the pedagogical documentation and within this book. We are deeply grateful for their artistic contributions.

We thank Leslie Prpich for her outstanding editing of the book; her insightful comments and encouraging support propelled us forward. Her expertise not only enhanced our English prose but also preserved the inherent beauty of the Spanish language.

Lastly, this book would not have been possible without the generous funding provided by the Canadian Social Sciences and Humanities Research Council, York University, and Western University.

# PEDAGOGIES OF PROXIMITY

# 1 The Itinerant School: Pedagogies of Proximity in Viral Times

In March 2020, the COVID-19 pandemic brought the world to a halt. Around the globe, schools closed, and most children experienced school from a distance. But in Cuenca, Ecuador, the young children of Santana Children's City, an elementary school, gathered in nine home gardens. These gardens comprise the itinerant school.

At a time when a global health crisis has challenged the usual close relations of a school, the itinerant school reimagines school relations. Multiple proximities and pedagogies of emergence abound. Children's and teachers' relations with the city's river, soil, chickens, worms, spiders, mountains, and more take centre stage. On a rainy morning in the itinerant school, for instance, a group of children in one home garden crowds around a flock of chickens, their attention focused on the birds' peculiar walk. Other children in another garden help the owner of an old clay oven coax it back to life. Elsewhere a group of children attends to everyday encounters with a river's ebbs and flows, while another cluster of children imagines a collective life in the underworld. Other children draw a centipede that has become their daily companion. Yet another group sings to the dead, having fashioned a clay vessel for a dead chick's journey to the afterlife. Through different practices, encounters, and modes of engagement, the teachers of the itinerant school make curriculum together with children and the gardens' inhabitants. Together with Alex Berry and Alicja Frankowski, we – Cristina and Veronica – participate as researchers through weekly virtual conversations with the teachers. Collectively, we carefully study what is emerging in each garden, and we speculate what might be possible.

For the past seven years we have been working on a research project in Cuenca, as part of the Climate Action Childhood Network (2024), in collaboration with teachers, children, and families of Santana: Ciudad de los Niñxs (Santana Children's City). In these years we have been thinking together and reconceptualizing what is possible in the education of young children in Andean Ecuador, which is Cristina's home. The itinerant school is part of our collaboration.

Cuenca is a city in the Ecuadorian Andes that spreads across an uneven geography surrounded by mountains that touch big, fast-moving clouds. The city is crossed by four rivers that follow intricate paths as they descend from the very tops of these mountains. The waters of these rivers are in deep relation with the clouds and the rain that form from condensed fog and mist emerging and coming up from the jungle. Located outside Cuenca city centre, Santana is a local private school that is surrounded by little creeks, the remaining of Andean forests that mix with colonial presences of eucalyptus, and a long history of many small artisanal and family-owned brick-making businesses. This complex geographical and cultural landscape has been a primary driver of our pedagogical work with Santana (http://riverplasticities.climateactionchildhood.net/). When the COVID-19 pandemic was declared, we were in the middle of our fourth year of intense, generative work with teachers and children from Santana's preschool, kindergarten, and first grade.

Ecuador, like most of the world, was burdened by the uncertainty and vulnerability that emerged during the pandemic. As the country went through those first waves of doubt and confusion, we tried to figure out how we should continue with our lives in the midst of an epidemiological crisis. Perhaps more importantly for the purpose of this book, Ecuador followed the same direction as other countries regarding education. Decisions were made for schooling to continue without disruption as much as possible, keeping a sense of "business as usual." Staying faithful to the global neoliberal capitalist agenda, the first decisions the Ecuadorian government made were in tune with the established discourse that understands education as "a 'resource' to be used as part of the standing reserve in the game of national economic competition" (Peters & Humes, 2003, p. 432). Indeed, in the global neoliberal agenda, schools and teachers are just part of a well-oiled machine: the systemic assemblage that keeps the markets going, even when that might entail creating a fiction, as Phelan and Rüsselbæk Hansen (2021) point out:

> In Europe and North America, for example, it is seemingly expected that education – in its institutional form – will soon return to business as usual. That is perhaps why teachers have been encouraged to act in a customary fashion: prepare lectures and learning activities (now in digital form) and offer them remotely to ensure no student falls behind – the neoliberal logic

> of learning as production is maintained. From this perspective, we might claim that we find ourselves in a *fictional* state of exception in which much is still the same – that is, things function in typical neoliberal ways. (p. 19, emphasis added)

A fiction here refers to trying to maintain the established neoliberal order and its logics by controlling "any possibility of tension, disjuncture or fracture" (Phelan & Rüsselbæk Hansen, 2021, p. 20) and by feeding the illusion that the only option is to keep the machine of progress going. Yet amid this fiction, Latour (2020) writes, "we have actually proven that it is possible, in a few weeks, to put an economic system on hold everywhere in the world and at the same time, a system that we were told it was impossible to slow down or redirect" (para. 2). Similarly, Roy (2020) asserts that,

> unlike the flow of capital, this virus seeks proliferation, not profit, and has, therefore, inadvertently, to some extent, reversed the direction of the flow. It has mocked immigration controls, biometrics, digital surveillance and every other kind of data analytics, and struck hardest – thus far – in the richest, most powerful nations of the world, bringing the engine of capitalism to a juddering halt. Temporarily perhaps, but at least long enough for us to examine its parts, make an assessment and decide whether we want to help fix it, or look for a better engine. (p. 1)

In this way, it seems to us that the pandemic has been – paradoxically – both a conjecture for the intensification of neoliberal logics and an eventful opening for the possibility to interrupt such logics. It is this possibility for interruption that interests us in *Pedagogies of Proximity*. In this book, we share our experience of engaging with the pandemic as an interruption of the neoliberal and capitalist normative discourses and material practices that understand education – and the educational experience – as a service that must do its part to fuel the capitalist engine. For us, the pandemic offered an invitation to engage with a world in ruins – with all its vulnerability and unknownness – and offered an opening for intensifying thinking about education otherwise. Our response to that invitation and that opening was to create an itinerant school.

The itinerant school is the bringing forth of a school outside institutional walls. We refer to it as itinerant to denote its mobile condition and the ebbs and flows of its emergent character, which interrupts modern schooling's stagnation and representationalism. We use the term itinerant to highlight the school's implied sense of movement and wonderment and its transient nature: The itinerant school has no fixed destination or established routines. This is so not only because it unfolds outside of institutional walls but also because, in the gardens, no classroom infrastructure was recreated. From the outset, we refused traditional school configurations so that multiple pedagogical and aesthetical movements could become possible. It is a school that "gestated itself" as Duschatzky and Aguirre (2019) write in the epigraph of this book. As such, it has carefully attended to "the relations that constitute her." The itinerant nature of this school means that its pedagogical processes, trajectories, and articulations happen in many ways, through multiple and multilayered encounters, as it refuses to remain captive to neoliberal and capitalist education. This school is itinerant because, as the chapters in this book illustrate, its pedagogical and curricular processes appear in many different guises and emerge in relation to many different concepts, occasions, and forms. In fact, the itinerant school only comes into form as it connects to human bodies, materials, places, stories, animals, plants, rivers, concepts, and so on.

We begin this chapter by theorizing the making of the itinerant school as acts of refusal of the capitalist and neoliberal logics embedded within early childhood education. The second part of the chapter broadly introduces the itinerant school's pedagogical orientations and curricular trajectories, which we delve into in more depth in Chapter 2. The third part of the chapter describes the nine home gardens in which the school unfolded. While the itinerant school has closed, its pedagogies continue, full of life and offering much to think with as we *hacemos escuela* (make school) with the children, families, and teachers of Santana. To reflect how this work carries on, in this book, we use both past and present tense in talking about the school, its gardens, and its pedagogies. Finally, we end this chapter with some thoughts on the itinerant school as an inventive pedagogical proposition that, like most of our work, dreams of other educational worlds.

## Acts of Refusal: The Emergence of the Itinerant School

Santana, like most of the schools in Ecuador and around the world, moved into online teaching in outstandingly efficient ways. The research project we were working on at Santana was part of this move. This was not an easy process. For the previous four years, teachers, children, and we had been intentionally creating a pedagogical experience that focused on proposing curricular trajectories aimed at recovering situated relations with place and context that had become lost. Indeed, through pedagogies of paying attention, slowing down, and attuning through walks to the nearby rivers, mountains, and forests and by engaging with situated questions, we slowly started to recuperate relations with place as we pondered what kinds of worldly relations we wanted to create and sustain. Our pedagogical intentions also aimed at undoing the strong grab of child development and child-centred practices – and the alliance of these two behemoths with colonial and neoliberal capitalist logics (Vintimilla & Pacini-Ketchabaw, 2020).

In those first years, we had created careful and intense pedagogical processes that focused on dismantling the taken-for-granted developmental discourses that characterized Santana's educational experience – discourses that had contributed to creating a curriculum of fragmentation, distance, and assimilation that ignored the situatedness of the educational experience, as well as children's inheritances and entanglements with place. Concerned with the histories of colonial and ecological devastation that characterize Cuenca's geography, and drawing on an ethics of vulnerability, we highlighted the relations and codependencies between humans and more-than-humans to rethink the project of humanity, its current axiologies, and education's implication in this project (Walcott & Abdillahi, 2019). We were immersed in this rich work when the global pandemic was declared.

Within a few weeks of Santana's move to online education, we knew things were about to get very difficult. What we didn't expect was the strong refusal and protest that children enacted. Simply put, the children disliked the new educational experience. They could not abide online education and the contradictions it represented, which contrasted sharply with what we had been doing pedagogically before the pandemic.

We found ourselves not knowing how to proceed, and we stumbled along through those hard first months. When the school year ended, we met with the school's director, Pablo Crespo, who opened the meeting with a plea for a different pedagogical trajectory: one that would not be online. Using words that were steeped in radical listening to the resistance we had experienced, Pablo said to us: "We need to create a different school. Children have clearly told us what they want, and we need to respond. We need to respond differently."

The itinerant school is an (imperfect) ethical-pedagogical response to the children's refusal to play along with the neoliberal fiction of business as usual. It also responds to the pedagogy of the virus, which could be perceived as a call to invent alternative educational worlds rather than perpetuate the broken fiction of reproducing "normal" educational worlds. As Roy (2020) insists, "the rupture exists. And in the midst of this terrible despair, it offers us a chance to rethink the doomsday machine we have built for ourselves. Nothing could be worse than a return to normality" (p. 3).

Guided by the spirit of Roy's words amid the rupture they announced, the itinerant school explored and proposed pedagogies in viral times. Housed in backyards and gardens offered by families, it spread throughout nine neighbourhoods in Cuenca. In each of these gardens, a teacher and a group of young children aged 3 to 5 met three days a week. We carefully created curricular processes that responded to the singular configuration of each garden: to its history, its location in the city, the stories that might relate to its creation, and the different relations it sustains. For example, if thinking about literacies, it would be literacies that emerged in the encounter between the children and the garden. The remaining two days of the week were completely dedicated to working with documentation and making pedagogical decisions focused on nourishing the unfolding curricular processes. This radical educational response instantiated generative pedagogical and curricular trajectories for pandemic living.

Perhaps the itinerant school, as our collective response to viral times, can be positioned in the realm of what Stengers (2015) refers to as the celebration of an event. She describes "having generated witnesses who learn to recount what they owe to [the event], what it has taught them, how it united them, how it forced them to learn from one another" (p. 155). The itinerant school as an event became, for the educators and the children (and for us), an experience "that signals the achievement of new connections between politics and an experimental, always experimental, production of a new capacity to act and to think" (Stengers, p. 155). The itinerant school has given us all an opportunity to do education in a different key – an almost unrecognizable key.

## Moments of Pedagogical Ideation and Proposition in Response to Viral Times

The itinerant school was born out of the need to reconsider education during the pandemic – and a wish to view the pandemic as an opportunity, a portal that allowed us to experiment with a different idea of schooling. It is important to highlight that, for us, the itinerant school did not substitute traditional forms of schooling, nor did it seek a redemptive version of schooling. This school was created *in* and *for* viral times: It responded to the conditions in which we were living in that unprecedented moment. Referring to pandemic times as an opportunity does not mean erasing the significant suffering and difficulty the pandemic brought. Instead, we learned with what the moment gave us. We created with and in response to the pandemic, and we did this as the ideation of a particular pedagogical individuation and imagination. These were crafted in an ongoing response to viral times. As we elaborate more deeply in Chapter 2, we approach ideation as acts that compose situations that bring something different in the curricular life of a school or an early childhood centre. This approach requires a collective intention to carefully attend to what is emerging and, through that attention, to insert a proposition that holds the potential to bring our attention onto something that might shift our field of perception.

The pedagogical propositions at the heart of this book are not offered as the premises for a pedagogical approach or a model but as a situated educational response to the conditions in which Santana found itself in the first wave of the COVID-19 pandemic. Our intention was not to adjust the mode of delivery of early childhood education so that we could continue with "business as usual." Rather, our intention was to take up a pedagogical gesture that turned our attention toward creating a different educational experience that afforded an alternative perceptual field. Experimentally we – teachers, children, families, and researchers – remade schooling by inventing other ways of doing education: an education that foregrounds and actively engages with temporal, spatial, social, and material conditions with the pedagogical aim of interrupting neoliberalism's stronghold in educational discourses and its alliance with modern schooling. Within an emergent alternative field of perception, we (the participating children, teachers, families, and researchers) reencountered ourselves and the world.

Next, we share some of the initial *knots of attention* that oriented our ongoing ideation and initial propositions across the gardens. These knots of attention were then taken up in the differentiation of each garden. They went through the continuities and discontinuities that portray inventive pedagogical work. We have written about them in the past tense, but they could equally be read in the present tense as a way to evoke the generative overflowing of possibilities that this school has brought to us as researchers. These initial ideations helped compose around and with the contingencies of each garden as we attended and attuned with what emerged. These ideations exist in deep, lively connection to the pedagogical orientations we describe in Chapter 2.

The itinerant school created a convivial meeting space that proposed experiences focused on weaving situated bonds and relationships among children. It did this at the same time we all lived and felt the difficulties and consequences of physical distancing, of inhibiting our expressions of affection, and of experiencing control in spontaneous encounters.

In the itinerant school, children engaged in educational actions and complex processes situated in each encounter's multiple expressions. These processes were created in relational attentiveness, with care and caring for what emerged in each garden and for the generative indeterminacies of those emergences.

The itinerant school connected to the difficulties the virus presented. In fact, the school emerged from the idea that children could perceive and feel the state of exception in which we were living and were collectively capable of making sense of it. Children were invited to respond to the difficult situations that arose. Thus, the school – together with children, teachers, and families – generated emergent and creative responses in daily living: Adults and children were jointly thinking *in* and *with* arising situations. The itinerant school considered children and teachers as active creators of a collective that maintained and nurtured their lively interactions and, at the same time, fostered conditions for otherwise affects and relationships to emerge. These affects and relationships connected children with the garden and with the multispecies that make their surroundings, as well as with their stories. The singularity of the itinerant school was made in this collective of multiple and interdependent presences. This collectivity reminds us of Manning (2013) when she writes: "The collective does not emerge after individuation: it is not the result of a process. It is the force of the process itself: all individuation is collective" (p. 353). The itinerant school spun a responsive curriculum that responded, in viral times, to children's desires to meet with others, share curiosities, initiate new games through mutual gestures, and invent ideas that, although they might be labelled as *ridiculous* or *childish*, needed to be valued as propositions for alternative possibilities. As we describe in the chapters of this book, in each of the gardens we experienced an abundance of theories, questions, propositions, and affective moments that emerged from the teachers' and children's proximity with each other and the life of the garden. Many of these emergent theories, questions, and propositions became the enabling force toward new forms of relationality with self, others, and that specific place.

## Pedagogical Documentation in the Itinerant School

In the itinerant school, we approached the practice of pedagogical documentation (Rinaldi, 2021) as the driving force of inquiry and curriculum making. Throughout the school year, in collaboration with the teachers, we created spaces for provocative and collective paying attention, attuning, thinking, and doing with what emerged as we found our way in and within what addressed us. We carefully documented these acts of attention, these thinkings and doings, and we created provisional pedagogical descriptions (through notetaking, photographing, videotaping, and sketching) to propel further affective attentiveness, thinkings and doings. The pedagogical documentation is curated on a bilingual Spanish and English website (http://viraltimes.climateactionchildhood.net/) that complements the discussion in this book. We invite readers to visit the website and to read Chapters 3 to 11 alongside the pedagogical documentation, which includes visuals and details of the happenings in each garden. The itinerant school intensified our ongoing thinking and pedagogical conceptualizations of documentation as a key practice in nondeterministic approaches to education and curriculum making. In Chapter 2 we share the ideas around doing documentation that took life in the midst of the creative and multilayered dynamics of our work alongside teachers and children.

The documentation in the website and the book is interrelated, not only geographically but conceptually. The pedagogical work comes together through the concepts of proximity and encounters. We invite readers to view this documentation mosaic both as individual pieces and by tracing their interrelated echoes.

For us, it is important to mention again the incomplete character of each documentation. This incompleteness reflects the ongoing process that each educator experienced in figuring out the process of making curriculum, nourishing ideas, proposing situations, and finding ways to cultivate emergence in a novel fashion. We intentionally want to work with incompleteness (and make it explicit) by attending to some of the not-yet-activated processes that become visible in the documentation. We do this by making speculative drawings of what could have been done but was not. We think of this speculative work with Stengers (2017), who writes: "speculative thinking aims at maximizing friction with experience, refusing the right every specialized thought grants itself: to explain, while eliminating anything that cannot be framed by the explanation" (p. 16). These drawings are visible as speculative supplements – not explanations – that are added in specific sections of the documentation. This is a gesture that projects into a possible future by hinting into a trajectory that *could have been* proposed and taken up.

## Pedagogical Orientations in the Itinerant School

By wanting to challenge the neoliberal tendency to abstract subjects from spatial, temporal, and social-material contexts (Roberts-Holmes & Moss, 2021), the itinerant school took seriously Cuenca's geographies and histories. Taking a cue from the region's ancestral practices of weaving, the itinerant school was carefully weaved through the histories and geographies of the home gardens and their unique neighbourhoods. We thoughtfully sustained situations that helped us to encounter, relate to, and cultivate the memories and presences that made each of the gardens unique. Indeed, each garden became a space for turning children's attention toward enlivening relations that were unfamiliar and outside the taken-for-granted themes that early childhood education has become accustomed to. In this way, we created pedagogical processes that allowed us to be present in place encounters that would touch us, surprise us.

Speaking back to neoliberalism's radical abstraction or its inclination to cease relational ties in favour of flexibility (Adams et al., 2019), we oriented ourselves pedagogically toward the concept of proximity. In other words, as we discuss in Chapter 2, proximity served as the pedagogical catalyst the itinerant school experimented with. Inspired by Todd (2015), we worked with the idea that "proximity is not solely about a fixed spatial distancing but about the movement inherent in approaching the [human and more-than-human] other" (p. 249). Thus, in each garden, educators and children encountered, through a variety of gestures and movements of approximation, not only each other (through sharing experiences) but also the garden and its inhabitants. This work in each garden engaged with particular questions: What might encountering each other and the world during the pandemic do? How might these encounters transform education, us, and those around us? What responsibilities are ushered in by proximity?

Importantly, in each garden, we carefully sustained situations that helped us to encounter and relate to the presences, histories, and memories that singularly made each garden and to slowly cultivate different educational and aesthetical experiences. Across the gardens, these encounters became the occasions for relational logics that interrupted the normative patterns of relations perpetuated by schooling and its alliance with modernity, an alliance that, as we know too well, reduces the multiplicity of onto-epistemologies – and their relational manifestations – to one normative genre of being human (McKittrick, 2015). It is exactly this alliance that the pedagogies of proximity we weaved in the itinerant school slowly unravelled. The itinerant school opened up possibilities to undo (even if momentarily) the human coded as white, rational, autonomous man and its sovereign self. Each garden (as Chapters 3 to 11 relate) became a space for turning children's attention toward enlivening relations that were unfamiliar and outside the taken-for-granted human subject that modern school is accustomed to reproducing through its representative and deterministic curricular practices. The pedagogical processes emerging within the gardens allowed us (including children) to question ingrained perceptions and sensitivities toward the modern human and turn our attention instead toward encounters that would undo and even displace (again, even if only temporarily) bounded, rational, and deeply conscious notions of the human.

## Nine Gardens of the Itinerant School

In what follows, we historically and geographically situate each garden and describe the conceptual threads for each.

Situated on the right bank of the Tomebamba river, at the foot of the Palacio de Huayna Cápac in the "Pumapungo" area, is El Vergel garden. Vergel contains the tangible memory of a space for exchange and encounter that has always characterized the place we now call Cuenca. In Vergel are Inca, Cañari, and colonial ruins, representing the framework created by the Andes. This neighbourhood is also known as the Herrerías, which still preserves its traditional iron workshops from colonial times, when pack mules were used to move across the city. Nowadays, this small corner of Cuenca embraces the past and the present – iron workshops rise up and survive modern forms of production.

Chapter 3 discusses the pedagogical work in El Vergel garden. It focuses on how we encountered clay as the main medium to create pedagogies that helped us become close to Andean ancestral onto-epistemologies. These pedagogies allowed children to engage with the difficulties of living and dying. They created the conditions for children to narrate themselves and their relation to life and death in ways that troubled transcendence. Working with the concept of circularity invited the children to a greater proximity with the garden's space, inhabitants, and coexistences. We deepened our close encounters with the garden's inhabitants while we planted. Our hands touched the moist soil and were surprised by the many creatures they met. Little seeds were placed carefully in the soil while children shared stories of the life that might emerge. Pill bugs, or wood bugs, were very present in the garden. We noticed how they easily shifted from being spread out to rounding themselves up in tight balls. We noticed their symbiotic interaction with the light and the effect of light on their transformation. Children became curious about other circular forms that were present in many animals and plants in the garden, and our attention to circularity intensified through experimenting with it as a concept within circular ancestral economies.

The itinerant school worked in two gardens on Cabogana mountain: Cabogana and Tejar. Cabogana is part of the Andean range that embraces Cuenca. To get to Cabogana, you walk through roads that gradually rise, revealing complex landscapes full of contrast that form the city valley. Ancient villages teeming with tradition and memories (natural/cultural) line the slopes of Cabogana at the same time urban development grows and stifles its traditional rurality. Brick and tile kilns are intertwined with grocery stores, traditional and fast-food vendors, internet cafés, and a huge storage facility for one of the city's main shopping centres.

In Chapter 4, through a focus on how clay encounters bring us closer to the histories and memories embedded in the soil of Cabogana mountain, we engage with processes for opening multiple alternative temporalities to recognize soil as a pedagogical protagonist and medium. Soil turns our attention toward the interrelated concepts of transformation, embodiment, and memories. These concepts, in turn, allow us to experiment with the continuities and discontinuities within events and within the shape of memories and histories.

In Chapter 5 we turn to the pedagogical work in El Tejar garden, focusing on encounters with a flock of chickens. We intentionally move away from generic conceptualizations of chickens to create and attend to processes that bring us into encounters with each bird's singularity. Our pedagogical purposes focus on the difficulties that emerged in the attempts to encounter irreconcilable differences between chickens and humans. We notice shifts within – and continuities between – the notions of self and other. Through drawing, as a medium for paying attention, we engage with other logics of movement in order to embrace the puzzlements that emerge from the incommensurabilities between children's and chickens' lives.

Narancay garden is located on Cuenca's southwestern border. Narancay is a connector to other cities in the south of Ecuador. As a passageway to the south, the area has morphed from a tourist destination to a commercial hub, which has changed the geography of the place.

Chapter 6 recounts the work done in creating composting pedagogies in Narancay garden as an attempt to generate conditions for collective communities of multispecies to flourish. These pedagogies involve processes of paying attention, relearning, composing, and decomposing as we zoom in on encounters with invisible underground worlds and how we are connected to their many inhabitants. We do so by carefully noticing and working in speculative ways with the lively, ongoing movements that connect the under- and above-ground worlds in this garden. In Narancay garden, provoked by an underground life and tunnelling system, the children encountered bacteria, fungi, and earthworms and imaginatively speculated about the many lives one can't see even though they sustain us. Using pastels, watercolours, and soil as languages for finding and tracing pathways, we reconfigured relational logics by animating the creatures of the soil.

Challuabamba neighbourhood is situated where Cuenca's city valley ends and the highland mountains begin; it is a meeting place of temporalities and existences. Here, Cuenca's expanding contemporary suburbia meets longstanding Andean farmlands. The Pan-American highway moves through Challuabamba, edging both ultramodern concrete housing developments and traditional adobe homes made of clay and grass. Challuabamba is figured by the meeting of these contradictory coexisting Andean realities.

Chapter 7 sketches the pedagogical work in Challuabamba garden. Children and educators gestured toward the difficulties of undoing the able-normal-independent human. Through processes of storytelling, invention, and reinvention, they reconfigured human existence by following children's invention of a human living underneath the world. Painting, drawing, sculpting, and shadow making provided pedagogical possibilities for blurring human exceptionality and noticing unthinkable collaborations between perceived separate beings.

The itinerant school worked in two gardens in the San Joaquín neighbourhood: San Joaquín of the Weavers garden and Yanuncay garden. San Joaquín's landscape presents two disparate worlds; traditional agricultural areas contrast with newly built modern homes often enclosed in gated communities. Here, multiple generations of basket weavers and other traditional artisans continue to make a living as their land is transformed aesthetically. San Joaquín is made out of the contrast that emerges in the encounter of these divergent worlds: the beautiful green farm fields and the manicured home gardens. A short stroll from this neighbourhood brings one to the Yanuncay river that, together with the Tomebamba river, runs down from higher elevations in the Andes. The Yanuncay is commonly known as the least altered of Cuenca's four rivers. However, at a closer look, the river has been reconstructed with impermanent stone borders that channel water to the local farms and artisans. Through these channels, the river provides for communities in myriad ways.

Chapter 8 traces the pedagogical work in San Joaquín of the Weavers garden. Children and educators focused on processes that enabled proximity with spiders and their dwellings. Pedagogically, we sought to unsettle ideas of the technocratic human as the sole maker of the world and drew instead on the work of spiders and on ancestral weaving to reconfigure our relationships with human agency to imbue them with humility. Spiderwebs became the site for attending to the complexities and sophistication spiders display in making their world.

In the pedagogical work in Yanuncay garden, described in Chapter 9, children and educators focused on river-light relations using simulation as a pedagogical concept and curricular process. Moving between multiple encounters with the river and our reanimations, we blurred the lines between magic and reality, natural and unnatural, bodies and shadows. This project brought us close to pedagogical processes that enact logics based not in duality and fragmentation but in attentiveness to the fluid properties of the river and the light that this garden is in relation with and depends upon.

Puertas del Sol garden shares its name with the neighbourhood where it is located. Puertas del Sol still holds vestiges of its history as a rural area that was built around and in relation to the Tomebamba river. The *haciendas* (plantations) of the past painted Puertas del Sol's landscape in monochromatic shades of carefully cultivated fields. In the last twenty years, its geography has been radically altered and forced to accommodate the demographic demands that press on Cuenca. Puertas del Sol's metamorphosis has been shaped by an agglomeration of small, gated communities and mid-size buildings that compete on who offers the best views to their dwellers. Although this area of Cuenca has suffered profound transformation, its active population still coexists in deep relation with the ever-changing water flows of the Tomebamba river.

Chapter 10 recounts the pedagogical work in Puertas del Sol garden, where children and educators came into close proximity with the Tomebamba. Although the river is geographically a central presence in Cuenca, a close relationship with the Tomebamba is often taken for granted. Children in Puertas del Sol encountered the singularity, history, complexities, contradictions, and toxic and nontoxic relations that make this river. Through multiple mediums (textile, charcoal, watercolours), we connected with the Tomebamba's sounds, fluidity, languages, memories, absences, and presences, which, in turn, invited us to think about the river's singularities and the different ways in which the Tomebamba exists in relation to water, trees, people, and stones. Through these encounters, children not only became close to the river but also speculated on what they share with the Tomebamba.

In Las Cholas de Piedra, waters from the high mountain lakes of El Cajas National Park move with the great Machangara river to the Machangaracocha lagoon. The Machangara river channel threads through the neighbourhood hills, paralleling three other lively rivers that flow to a valley that shapes the city of Cuenca. A central figure in this place is a monument called Las Cholas de Piedra (in English, stone dolls), a symbol of mestizo (mixed) Andean subjectivity and the important work of women, *cholas cuencanas*, that characterize both this countryside community and the city below.

Chapter 11 sketches the pedagogical work in Las Cholas de Piedra garden. Children noticed traces of others who were once in the garden but have disappeared. Using yarn as a language to think with/through, we encountered white feathers and empty webs that birds and spiders had left behind. We intentionally created pedagogical processes to think together about what might be required for their return. Yarn became the material language that gave us the grammars to knit together stories and correspondences among children, educators, absent creatures, and ancestral presences.

We have reluctantly included a concluding chapter. We say reluctantly for two reasons: first, because the ideas we shared are not final and, second, because we always try to avoid the move towards applicability that, in our experience, is common in the field of early childhood education. The conclusion in this book is not a place to search for directives or defined guidelines. It was written in the spirit of the itinerant school, which is that of a conceptual ongoingness and inventive pedagogical processes that are highly situated and that aim to destabilize and shift normative modern representational ontology and epistemology.

## Education in an Unrecognizable Key

In the pandemic postscript to their book denouncing neoliberalism in early childhood education, Roberts-Holmes and Moss (2021) suggest that "now is the time for a radical re-thinking of education freed from the constraints imposed by neoliberalism, a 'Great Reset' that starts with deliberating on the purposes of education" (p. 181). Perhaps some might think of the itinerant school as a great reset, but we propose it, instead, as an educational experiment. In an educational experiment, Duschatzky (2016) explains,

> exchanges are laborious and uncertain. There is no plan to reproduce, no tabula rasa on the other side, no mouldable body; there are signs, signals, forces, modes of perception, tones, affectivities, sensitivities, experiences that become the subject of questioning, and components that intervene in the peculiarities that the exchanges will take. (p. 25, our translation)

At the itinerant school, we laboured through uncertain exchanges and encounters to leave behind the known language and point of view of the neoliberal early childhood school. We left behind the recognizable by affirming its centrality, its failures, its history, its achievements, its functions, and its conflicts. In some ways, we cannot talk about the itinerant school as a school. Inspired again by Duschatzky, we might say that the itinerant school is simply what moved in a certain constellation of forces or what happened at the very instant in which the pandemic caught us off guard and opened us to interrogating the ways in which we were being affected.

What follows in this book is a recounting of what took place pedagogically and curricularly in each garden. To this end, pedagogies of proximities are different in each garden; they are never one thing, never have a consistent form. They constantly displace themselves. By definition, they are itinerant. The very nature of the itinerant school compels our pedagogical work to take on other forms that will continue to alter as we envision alternative educational worlds with children and teachers in Cuenca.

# 2 Co-presence and Proximity

The stories and micro-experimentations we share in this book are about the careful and intense pedagogical work that transpired in the itinerant school. As we mentioned in Chapter 1, we were seeking an alternative pedagogical "capacity to act and to think" (Stengers, 2015, p. 155) amid a pandemic. In the first main section of this chapter, we describe some of the generative ideas and pedagogical orientations that at times interfuse and at other times sustain and even agitate the stories and micro-experimentations included in the following chapters. In the second section, we share our work and ideas around pedagogical documentation, the key practice for curriculum making in the itinerant school.

## Two Realizations

The pedagogies in viral times that characterize the itinerant school were crafted as ethico-pedagogical responses to two main realizations. The first, as we mentioned in the previous chapter, was the children's refusal of online schooling and its implied fiction of an educational experience that should continue "as usual." The second realization was one we have been grappling with for many years in our work: that we are amid and within a necessary onto-epistemological shift. Baixauli (2023) helps to put a precise point on this:

> The composition of the world we inhabit has mutated, as well as the relationship between its various worlds, since the advent of the New Climate Regime. The earth has begun to show that it was never something inert and entirely appropriable – as modernity thought and treated it – but that it also has agency. Climate change and the pandemic force us to situate ourselves as modes of existence among other modes of existence, human

> and nonhuman, in mutual dependence on our respective worlds. (p. 12, our translation)

For us, the spread of COVID-19 magnified this shift and heightened our awareness that we exist in deep and complex interdependence with the planet, other humans, and more-than-human actors. We are in constant proximity, correspondence, and interrelation. We could say that the pandemic highlighted what many feminist and postcolonial theorists have argued for decades: that we become in relational entanglement. As Ingala (2023) writes, "Every identity, every substance, every essence (and therefore every individual) is nothing but the result of a network of relations that constitute and sustain it (or dismiss it and let it fall)" (p. 61, our translation). These realizations constantly met the urgency we encountered in what we recognize as a paradoxical viral pedagogy. There is an urgency to do everything possible to stay alive and, at the same time, to find new ways to make sense, to rethink what has been taken for granted, and to think other forms of relations and community. The pedagogical paradox of the "communovirus" (Nancy, 2021) both points to the vulnerability of our lives and invites us to *establish life* (Esposito, 2021) by proposing alternative possibilities. Taking up this paradox, in the itinerant school we imagined alternative educational possibilities that were, actually, a situated response to viral times, allowing us to enact pedagogical work that has the capacity to act and think (Stengers, 2015). Thus, while the children's refusal of online schooling was the initial provocation to imagine creating an educational experience beyond the traditional classroom and in neighbourhood gardens, the insistent onto-epistemological provocation required our deep attention and dedication toward inventing pedagogical processes and understandings that aim to destabilize and shift normative, taken-for-granted modern representational ontology and epistemology.

## Between Realizations: A Pedagogical Trajectory

The itinerant school actively unsettled modern schooling and its (usually) tacit commitment to perpetuate representational epistemologies. As educational scholars have pointed out, despite strong challenges to representational epistemology in the last two centuries, schooling is still organized around this representational view of knowledge, and the school from which the itinerant school emerged was certainly no exception to this lineage. Representational or true knowledge, as Biesta and Osberg (2007) write, "is supposed to accurately signify something that is present and this something is independent reality" (pp. 17–8).

In this understanding, school becomes, at best – or in its less punitive and supposedly more progressive instance – a space where children make meaning of the simplified representations of a world they are separated from. This is a world to which we often refer in education as "the real world" (code perhaps for the labour market). The more that modern society separates children from the world, the more schooling takes on the task to teach young people *about* the world and how they are separated from it (Biesta & Osberg, 2007). Our experience in the itinerant school troubled representation by considering not only onto-epistemological questions but also those of purpose and value (axiological) that, ultimately and persistently, unsettle the very idea of modern schooling (as *about* and *for* the world rather than *of* it).

We situate our pedagogical practice as a gesture towards nonrepresentational pedagogies that do not think of schooling as attempting to provide children with knowledge or facts about an objective and independently existing world. We view children as deeply embedded in a relational world "where knowledge is not a reflection of a static world but emerges from our engagement with the world" (Biesta & Osberg, 2007, p. 28). This is why our efforts were driven by an idea of education that is interested in staging situated curricular processes that are highly emergent and relational and in pedagogical practices that put forward different modes of engagement and relational thinking. This is an idea that makes us less interested in the representation and repetition of established educational worlds and much more committed to creating evental conditions for *otherwise* educational worlds, where humans are envisioned in constant "relations of modification and reciprocity" (Anderson & Harrison, 2016, p. 9) and where all action is interaction taking place in multiple encounters within and with the world.

We intentionally decided not to reproduce the aesthetics of a school in the garden. School aesthetics, with their desks and structures, are embedded in the representational and hierarchical onto-epistemologies typical of modern schooling. These aesthetics position subjectivities and what is possible to think and create even before anyone enters the educational space. Also, these are aesthetics organized around a focus on knowledge transmission and comprehension. Our interest in the itinerant school was to gesture towards thinking schooling differently during the pandemic. Such a move requires more than simply changing the organization of the classrooms into a "provisional space" where we do the same as was done before. Thus, honouring the children's refusal and heeding a critical call, we leave the Ecuadorean programmatic curriculum behind us (without ignoring it) and create an itinerant school addressing the very problem of encountering and being in proximity within the gardens.

## Encounters and Proximity

Holding close these considerations and realizations, we enter the gardens with deep curiosity and attentiveness towards the multiple encounters that might emerge, aware also of the challenges and possibilities of proximity. *Pedagogical encounters* and *proximity* become the two orienting concepts for our pedagogical processes and curriculum making. Yet these are *not* two preformed concepts selected for pedagogical application. That is, we do not begin with a definition of terms that the teachers are then able to apply in each garden. We approach the concepts as experiences to inhabit, to attune to, and in which to initiate and provoke educational processes. In this regard, we are inspired by the invitation of Todd (2003) to stage pedagogical encounters as a way of "creating conditions for ethicality, as they promote conditions for being, both of which involve relationships between self and Other" (p. 29) – and we extend the category Other to the more-than-human. We are also inspired by the idea that "one cannot think proximity's experience but it is proximity that forces us to think" (Libertson, 2012, p. 119) and that – as an experience – proximity entails communication and coexistence with another that *we do not fully comprehend*.

In the gardens, our focus is on the proximities between the children, teachers, and the gardens' many inhabitants (plants, insects, flowers, water, trees, chickens, spiders, birds, clay, and so on). These elements bring forward moments of communication marked by incommensurability, the impossibility of being indifferent to each other – an impossibility afforded by proximity – as well as resistance to thinking of communication as a means to grasp and know. In the itinerant school, communication is never reduced to comprehension. Proximity offers an approach into each other's presence, which, to our surprise, creates effects that go beyond understanding.

In these moments we learn to pay attention to the multiple *exchanges of impressions* that give life to the different stories that emerge in each garden. Proximity invites us to prioritize our pedagogical attention towards the in-between space of an encounter, the not (yet) known, the (im)possible, the unconscious, the otherwise. Pedagogically, this is very significant. We are well aware that, often, pedagogical encounters tend to reduce alterity (e.g., between child and animal or educator and curriculum) to the dimensions of the same (a given understanding, a safe bet), or rather, the focus tends to be on the transmission of meaning making, a kind of circuit of exchange of accepted significance. Instead, moments in proximity incite us to resist these familiar tendencies. We ask instead how we might nurture processes that keep alive the alterity of (and within) relations? What compositions (of materials, of situations, of dynamics, of temporalities) might help us to keep (and even highlight) the interval created by difference within the ensemble of relations that emerge in the gardens? What might the implications for educational experiences be if we consider proximity as "a non-indifference towards alterity" (Libertson, 2012, p. 200) where "Alterity is not another Same" (p. 203)? And, how do we nurture communality in a way that ideas and emotions are transformed? These questions push our pedagogical intentions to focus more on matters of communication and mutual contamination. They also invite teachers to resist an interest in content-knowledge and its totalizing forces, which so often characterize the education of young children.

In the itinerant school, we propose proximity as communication and thus as what creates *acts of involvement* which, in turn, incite our mutual abilities to respond. Proximity is the experience of being involved, being in complex relationality, being entangled. It is not homogenizing because proximity keeps the necessary relational distance alive in and as alterity. We end this section with a question that has emerged in different moments in the itinerant school. This is a question that we still carry and share in the welcome of the ongoingness of this work: What might be possible if education were preoccupied with questions of proximity alongside (or even instead of) questions of comprehension?

The pedagogies in the itinerant school challenge the cognitive-rational and predefined character of education's strong instrumentalism. To do so means working with pedagogies that attend to the *field of emergence* that exists in any educational context. Doing this means challenging a Western understanding of knowledge as preorganized and static, where children are to be filled with information as if they are empty vessels. Instead, attending to emergence demands working with knowledge more as "finding a way" (Manning, 2016, p. 7). Thus, we refer to our work in the itinerant school as *haciendo escuela* (making school) to indicate the relational space of emergence and its demand for pedagogical attention. In response, it becomes an *attention* that is not *to* "but rather is with and toward, in and around" (Manning & Massumi, 2014, p. 4). To make school is to co-compose "an experience in the making" (p. 5). At the same time, emergence is not a space of sheer exploration where anything goes, and we do not only follow children's leads. We do not refer to these pedagogies as those that follow individuals' interests (Nxumalo et al., 2018). Teachers and children share attentiveness toward generative unfolding – its latency – and what is taking place in the manifold and multiple encounters in which they participate, in the in-between space of these encounters. As we have seen in other projects (Pacini-Ketchabaw, Kocher, & Kind, 2024; Vintimilla, 2020; Vintimilla & Kind, 2021), in the itinerant school, it is the *co-compositional space* that *calls in* pedagogical attention and not the isolated child, not the teacher, and not the more-than-human. In pedagogical work, multiple practices support and enable this attentiveness and attunement. In the itinerant school, the main practice for doing so is pedagogical documentation. But for us, this does not mean or imply *making meaning* of children's ideas. In the itinerant school, pedagogical documentation is a significant practice for emergence.

### Pedagogical Documentation in the Itinerant School: From Meaning Making to World Making

Although we appreciate pedagogical documentation's widely accepted definition as a practice that makes children's learning and meaning making visible (Bombino, 2010; Edwards et al., 2011; Giamminuti, 2009; Krechevsky et al, 2013; Wien, 2013), we approach documentation less as a practice of making meaning and more as one (among many possible pedagogical practices) for world making. In our attempt to resist representational logics, this distinction matters. We make this shift so that we can participate in and emphasize pedagogical work that engages with knowledge as implicated, entangled, imperfect, and messy rather than detached, graspable, and consumable. We do documentation as a pedagogical practice of world making because we do not conceptualize the world as an object for our understanding and meaning making. We carefully attend to encounters in a relational space, to the different ways in which we are addressed in these encounters by/with others (humans and more-than-humans) and to the multiple (often indiscernible) makings that we slowly co-compose and assign collective significance to. These makings are world making because they attempt to insert *a difference that makes a difference* and not just repeat the educational worlds we are given. Manning (2016) writes that "what a child asks is not that we define experience in advance, but that we make it" (p. 8). We agree! We further propose that we do so, not only because the child asks, but because that is actually what pedagogical work is about.

To practice documentation as world making is not easy. It is an inventive-creative practice and not a formula. It is a practice that asks us to risk our modern attachments to mastery, control, and predictability and to consider pedagogical work as imaginative and speculative.

Next, we offer four ideas on documentation as world making that leaked out from our practicing, thinking, and noticing the movements of our thoughts as we engaged with this form of documentation in the itinerant school.

### *Documentation as a Practice for Emergence*

Documentation as world making is a pedagogical practice linked to an understanding of pedagogy as living knowledge that emerges in the thinking and creating of educational situations and projects. Thus, for us, documentation is not a practice to facilitate a more engaging learning experience within a predefined educational project. It is not a practice designed for deterministic or representational pedagogies. Nor is it a stand-alone practice without any link to pedagogy and pedagogical work. For us, documentation is a pedagogical practice for ideating on the basis of what emerges within the *specificity* of educational situations and projects. This is why, in the itinerant school, we approach pedagogical documentation as a practice that attends to the multiple encounters that take place in each garden.

We use the concept of a *field* inspired by Eco (1962/1989), who writes: "the notion of field is provided by physics and implies a revised vision of the classic relationship posited between cause and effect as a rigid one-directional system: now a complex interplay of motive forces is envisaged, a configuration of possible events, a complete dynamism of structure" (p. 9). We are particularly interested in educational spaces as this dynamic space of co-composition and encounter. For us, this is a participatory mediatic space where documentation is approached as a driving interpretative practice that begins in not knowing and that follows and attunes to what is emerging in movement, its tensions, its impasses, and its revelations.

### *Documentation as Work in Movement*

Documentation as a practice for world making is work in movement. The different educational fields of emergence where we work are not neutral or ahistorical. They reflect often multiple and contradictory onto-epistemologies that are sometimes hard to reconcile. It is within these uneven fields, however, that we create movement and dynamism as necessary conditions for possible onto-epistemological reconfigurations to emerge within the encounters.

Throughout the itinerant school, we have created spaces for tracing temporary ideas, ideas in movement, and propositions. We carefully document thinkings and doings while introducing modifications and interferences into them. We curate provisional pedagogical descriptions to propel further thinking and doings. Here, it is important to clarify that we do not understand documentation as merely the creation of descriptions or representations of what was significant, even though it has a descriptive character. Instead, we understand documentation as a pedagogical practice that answers or responds to what was significant.

Understanding documentation as a work in movement highlights this *provisional character* as necessary and as a demand that comes from the emergent *indiscernible* and *indefinite* articulations typical of relational spaces in the making. These articulations permeate moments that are outside the realm of clarity, of knowing exactly what we are doing and where we are going within the relational and emergent field. Yet, these opaque articulations require pedagogical care, attention, and intention. Indefiniteness and indiscernibility are not easy expressions to work with in education, especially in a representational world where teachers are expected to know and effortlessly predict the aims of their work.

Amid this difficulty, we find a profound generative force in indefiniteness (Manning & Massumi, 2014) and indiscernibility. They are charged with the momentum and pedagogical energy of *suggestiveness* or what Eco (1962/1989) refers to as a "poetic of suggestiveness" that exists at the heart of articulations of the present. Suggestiveness is what stimulates pedagogical work to *project* and lean towards the future because it asks us to think *what if* and to consider what *might be*. Suggestiveness is a generative force that projects us into further interpretation and creation, indicating the pedagogical vitality of a project. Thus, suggestiveness calls on our ability to respond and to define some intentions that will continue giving form to the pedagogical work. These intentions are pedagogical thus they offer us an orientation or direction rather than setting an end goal. They involve an ability to envision, which is different from prediction. They open up pathways.

Suggestiveness sets up intentions that are more about stimulation and anticipation than predetermination. Suggestiveness stimulates and, at the same time, depends on teachers' and researchers' imaginative and affective interpretative resources (rather than persistent literalism) as it incites processes of ideation.

### *Documentation as a Practice of Attention and Ideation*

As a practice, pedagogical documentation demands attention and attunement to the ongoing, generative dynamic between the traces of what we find pedagogically significant within a process (Rinaldi, 2021) and the different propositions ideated on the basis of what we found significant. In other words, as we engage in documentation, we are moved by a set of pedagogical questions, concerns, and orientations that help to discern and give value to what happened at the same time they propel us into attending to and cultivating new forms of knowing, acting, and living, through processes such as questioning, fabulating, figuring out, enacting, inventing, trying out, daring, stumbling, to name a few. Hence, pedagogical documentation is a practice of pedagogical attention and creation that moves both retrospectively and prospectively. Here, it is interesting to notice that because it is retrospective, documentation has a descriptive character, yet, because it is prospective it has a transformative force. For us, the prospective aspect of documentation engages the practice of *projecting via ideation*. The intention is to purposefully activate and respond to the latency of ideas, possibilities, and affects through material, interpretative, and speculative processes of curriculum making. Acts of ideation compose situations that weave something different in the curricular fabric. This weaving is not a simple practice as it requires a collective intention to carefully attend to what is latent and, through that attention, insert a proposition that holds the potential to bring our attention onto something that might shift our field of perception. In other words, we could say that documentation as world making involves a double move: It creates particular educational experiences while simultaneously making sense of those experiences.

In the itinerant school, we engage in the process of ideating with teachers because we are *pedagogical projectists* (a translation of the Italian *progettisti*) who are interested (as ones who are in the midst of things) in curriculum making as that which enables new and alternative relational fields – ones that are less based in managerial logics, less humancentric, and less representational than are typically the case in education. As projectists we were inspired to "improvise a passage rather than to innovate with representations of the unforeseeable" (Gatt & Ingold, 2020, p. 145). In our case, we understand this inspiration as a desire for our ideations to provoke situated worlding stories that can be read as "epistemological metaphors" (Eco, 1962/1989, p. 3) and that can "constitute a new way of seeing, feeling, understanding and accepting the world, where [established/traditional] relations are broken and where – even though with difficulty – new relational possibilities are being delineated" (Eco, p. 3).

### *Documentation Involves Incompleteness and Openness*

Finally, and as a way of insisting, documentation, for us, enables and enriches our ability to envision pedagogically. That is, it is a practice that proposes inventive processes within an educational setting without fully knowing, without fully seeing, yet being moved by what we call *pedagogical prospectives* – which means pedagogically facing and engaging with a future we cannot predict and yet a future we dare to story. Thus, there is an openness and incompleteness in pedagogical documentation as world making.

This openness and incompleteness is reflected in the ongoing processes and trajectories of making curriculum: in nourishing ideas, in proposing situations, in attending to the intangible, and in finding ways to cultivate emergence in a novel fashion. It also reflects the multiplicity of meanings, the plurality of intentions, the interrelations, and the different ways of being that could take place but may not, reminding us that educational spaces are always bursting with potentiality even as they are also constrained. Recognizing this incompleteness is also a resistance to representational epistemologies and the predictable manner with which they organize knowledge and our relations within educational spaces and with the world.

In these ways, documentation as world making "forces us to turn once again toward the world for what it has to teach us" (Gatt & Ingold, 2020, p. 148). In doing so in the itinerant school, our pedagogical prospectives enact what Gatt and Ingold (2020) refer to as "prospective correspondences" (p. 148) among the children, teachers, and inhabitants in each of the gardens. These correspondences are steeped in documentation's acts of attentiveness. In them, we do not "attend to things only so far as it is necessary to accommodate them within the compartments of thought, so that they can be ticked off, accounted for, understood, laid to rest" (Ingold, 2023, p. 23) or to assess or to gather more information about the child or to collect "data." Rather, we are referring here to an attentiveness "to bring things to presence: not to discover the truth about them, but to discover the truth that comes from them, in the experience" (p. 23).

As you read each of the following chapters, we invite you to keep present the ideas we have offered in this chapter. We propose this because they hold the pedagogical and methodological vitality of this project. They speak of the educational and aesthetic possibilities that were gestated amid a pandemic, amid its vulnerabilities and emotions. They speak too of our commitment towards the children's refusal and their desire for a different education.

# 3 Circularity Is More than a Shape: El Vergel Garden

Figure 3.1. Speculative Drawing: El Vergel Garden

At the back of El Vergel garden is a clay studio that belongs to the family who lent the garden to the itinerant school. The children are inevitably attracted to the studio, which faces the garden. The garden bathes in Andean light and, wherever one turns, one finds multiplicity and colour. It is in this space that Valeria, the teacher, invites the children to gather, to find ways to meet and talk and to slowly create a collective meeting space. From the very beginning of the school year, the studio and clay become the gathering forces.

This chapter narrates eventful pedagogical processes in the curricular trajectories that unfold in El Vergel garden (http://viraltimes.climateactionchildhood.net/index.php/gardens/el-vergel-garden/clay-vessel/). The narratives focus on how children and educators encounter clay as a medium to bring into existence pedagogies that support children to inhabit Andean ancestral onto-epistemologies. These pedagogies allow the children to engage with the existential circularity of living and dying. Educators create the conditions for children to narrate themselves and their relations to life and death in ways that trouble transcendence without avoiding the difficulties that such an inquiry might bring. Working in El Vergel garden with the concept of circularity, these pedagogies invite children and educators to a greater proximity with the garden's space, inhabitants, and coexistences. In collaboration with educators, we not only inquire into the circular forms present in many animals and plants in the garden, we also intensify our attention to circularity by experimenting with it as a concept within alternative ancestral economies.

## Clay and Vessels

Clay as medium allows for a trace or a mark that speaks back to the children of their worldly presence, as if the pedagogy of clay is indicating that one is in/of the world: in dialogue, leaving traces, marking a presence and being momentarily and continually marked back. This is a collective making that happens around the very gathering force of clay – and beyond children's interests. Clay invites dynamic and reciprocal movements that appear harmonious yet chaotic: pokes, pinches, stamps, pressing of hands all happening at the same time. Through these small gestures a collective slowly takes shape in the space. This process is difficult. There is movement while order and control press against our thinking and speak against our common understandings of schooling – and to our assumptions about how teachers and children should engage in an educational space.

Without distancing ourselves from these difficulties, we notice them and purposely intensify these noticings, including children's movements, interactions, and encounters – and, at times, their chaotic energy. Through these processes of noticing and intensifying, Valeria transforms holes in the clay by naming them vessels. This naming, in turn, brings into presence the importance of clay vessels in Andean cosmologies. For Valeria, these tiny holes are earth-made vessels that evoke much more than the material itself. These vessels hold us all, or, as Valeria announces, bring children close to what she refers to as the Pachamama, a multifaceted concept encompassing the Andean world-view of nature as the source of life and as a dynamic entity embodying both material and spiritual dimensions. As holders, the vessels do not emerge "from nothing, but transform what is already there" (Arnold, 2019, p. 144). Bringing the vessels into the children's field of perception evokes Andean emphasis on transformation and on how materials are never only a material but participants in life making: "from clay to powder to paste and finally form in pottery making" (Arnold, p. 144). In the process of shaping vessels, Valeria "demands intertwined creative and social (learning and dissemination) processes where introducing life and personhood into material form is an integral aspect to be learnt" (Arnold, p. 144). Valeria is creating pedagogical processes that allow children to participate in new forms of signification and expand the value and recognition given to things and objects. In doing that, they collectively reposition our humanness.

Because these vessels are themselves life-given, they participate in story making, holding multiple histories and narratives. In thinking the vessels as containers and creators of stories, the children connect to ancestral memories and reshape them as they engage with the present. Stories are shared collectively, and in their sharing, children participate in nurturing a collective memory. Putting it differently, Valeria invites the children to see themselves as memory makers: As part of something woven collectively, the children retell ancestral memories that put the past into conversation with the contemporary. This is relevant to us because it invites the children to see themselves as a part of a memory that is presented not as a normative tale but as material for fabulating collective stories that have the potential to trouble liberal notions of the self-enclosed subject.

Rather than compartmentalizing knowledge and transitioning children from one bit of knowledge to another, Valeria works with the Andean idea of life in material form. She and the children spend time noticing the different forms that clay can have, barbotine (slip) being one of them. Dripping barbotine from a brush onto paper, children tell stories and experiment with symbols. We are careful not to collapse a moment like this into a recognizable experience of printmaking. We want to keep the liveliness of these acts of making a collective memory that is now enhanced with the production of its own symbology. We care for how a moment like this is a moment in the making of a we and of a common culture in an Andean garden. For us, what these processes might reveal is

> a perception of the world and the universe shaped by "dynamic processes of interactivity: complementary coexistence, division, encounter and investment" (Godenzzi, 2007a: 153). In this perspective, the relationality, expressed among other things by reciprocity, between the different elements of the universe establishes a circuit of transmission of the vital force between … them. We could say, using as a metaphor an important practice of Andean culture, that the universe is conceived as a kind of fabric composed of a multitude of elements, all directly or indirectly related to each other. (Beauclair, 2013, p. 45, our translation)

Following the idea of a complex weaving, as Valeria continues the work, the printed symbols take up new meanings and collective force as they are orally renarrated and exposed within the garden's collectivity. Attending to the multiplicity of the emerging stories that shape and nourish collective memories, Valeria and the children inaugurate a library composed of their colourful and lively clay-inspired visual journals.

The visual journals hold emerging clay stories that function as conduits to place-traditions. The library becomes a space for encounters and generates listening, questioning, and dialogue. Ideas and thoughts are exchanged, shared, and even contested within the garden. The garden evolves into a space where multiple understandings and voices encounter each other and create a common story. Relevantly, in this library Valeria purposely resists evaluating the visual journals as the children's ability (or lack thereof) to represent and reproduce information through practices of reading and writing. So much more is happening in this context: Children create texts that are taken seriously because they are assigned the capacity to mobilize meanings and knowledge produced in situ. Rather than conceiving reading and writing as practices of mere transmission or as knowledge that individual children acquire, these texts are seen as highly responsive and attuned with what is happening in the garden.

## Life and Death

Valeria cultivates spaces for dialogue intertwined with the making of clay vessels. Hands, clay, stories intermingle with a song she offers the children as she creates dynamic connections among different, yet interrelated, elements. This time it is *dia de los muertos* (day of the dead). Tuning into "*La Vasija de Barro*" ("The Clay Vessel") by Andrade (1950), whose lyrics evoke Inca burial rituals where clay vessels functioned as containers for the dead, the children listen attentively, with curiosity. Valeria makes space for the children's curiosities to emerge and be listened to. The song becomes an invitation to engage with death as a part of life. We, as teachers, navigate the tensions and vulnerabilities we feel when the children want to deepen the conversations about death. It is not easy to talk about death during a pandemic, yet at the same time, the children's willingness and desire to talk about death and life makes these conversations unavoidable. Their willingness also demonstrates to us the children's refusal to embody a naivety and innocence often assigned to children about death and dying. Valeria works carefully with what emerges. She pauses and creates a dialogical space with the children as an invitation to pay attention to what is emerging and pedagogically significant.

We are reminded of the work of Biesta (2017) where he writes that "the teacherly gesture … tries to say no more than 'look, there is something there that I believe might be good, important, worthwhile for you to pay attention to'" (p. xx). Such a gesture is possible when education is not reduced only to moments in learning but can be seen instead as an aesthetic experience that touches the soul (Biesta, 2017). By creating opportunities to experience and dwell on Andrade's lyrics, the children are invited to create their own connection with long-extinguished funeral practices – not to somehow adopt them but to create connections to the past and, importantly, to ceremonies.

Ceremony becomes a relevant practice in the making of the everyday of El Vergel garden. Its forms, protocols, and rituals bring a different way to relate to the passing of time and to how we come together in an educational space. Ceremony is created through an accumulation of interrelated elements: laying a circular piece of yellow fabric on the floor, creating a circle with the children, bringing the guitar, placing a firepit in the middle of the circle, singing, repeating "La Vasija de Barro" once, twice, three times. Here, ceremony is different from early childhood education's mechanistic repetition of activities for the sake of entertaining children. Nor can this encounter be interpreted as pretend play that prepares children for future performance in society. Ceremony in El Vergel is part of a ritual that is situated and collective. As the children and Valeria gather around the fire burning the clay vessels, they join their ancestors' rituals.

This ritual becomes the connector between two gardens when the children from El Tejar witness the death of a chick and, moved by their concern about burying it, reach out to the children of El Vergel to request a vessel for their chick. This connection becomes an opportunity to create dialogue between children in two different gardens, and it also intensifies our intention to create educational spaces that enact careful dialogues with the world. Children take the request very seriously as they ponder the questions they had posed about clay vessels for burials. They carefully experiment with potential designs that would hold the dead chick with dignity. We think about what is enabled in attending to death and dying in a pedagogical space. This is not just an abstract conversation with children about death; the children actively live death as a response in their lifeworlds. For El Vergel's children, dying is present in their lives, as is living. Death's presence is unmistakable. Our co-presence with death – our attending to this co-presence – also becomes a form of caring for life.

In other words, death, for the children, in their engagement with it, is far from dichotomous with life. For example, many of the vessel designs include corn seeds for the chick to take to its next life. The proximity between living and dying that this experience affords, and its intimate relation to the experience of the pandemic, is something these children are willing to explore. Furthermore, as we listen to their stories, we notice that, in many ways, the children's visions echo Andeans' temporal conceptualizations that position life and death as crucial "states of existence" (Klaus, 2019, p. 105). Within Andean cosmologies, death is not a termination but an alteration: "The dead [are] powerful animate beings who [continue to exert] influence in the living world" (Klaus, p. 105). Perhaps the plants, flowers, and corn seeds the children include in their burial designs echo Andeans' act of placing a corpse in a tomb, which Haagen Klaus suggests may be "conceptually akin to seed nurturance, cultivation, and human fertilization" (p. 105).

## Composing with Circularity

As children become witnesses of life emerging from the burial containers, Valeria takes up life's circularity as a concept to compose with pedagogically. For us, composing pedagogically means to speculatively arrange a set of elements (material, atmospheric, intellectual, social, aesthetic, etc.) within an experience as a way to attend to and care for ideas and situations that are charged and vibrant. These might be ideas and situations that are already formed but also ones that come alive through the process of composing. A pedagogical composition is irreducible to the mere sum of elements put together. It is the making of a relational field and the attentiveness to what emerges with it, as well as its excess, that matters pedagogically.

As Gose (2019) explores, "the circulation of life [is] a distinctive and enduring Andean cosmological concern" (p. 115), and that same concern becomes the driving force for El Vergel's remaining pedagogical processes. The Andean circulatory cosmos does not move through progression, but "new points of departure arise on the basis of established orders" (Gose, p. 126). This idea evokes our pedagogical work, which is committed to inserting something different into what is already established, not as an act of harmonization or totalization, but "as an encounter of elements, a composition of unequal and opposing elements" (Beauclair, 2013, p. 117, our translation). This composition attends to different elements; it crafts conditions; it creates intersections and uncommon coalescences that have ideating potential. Our ways of making curriculum are highly attuned to these forms of potentiality. For us, curriculum making is always a practice of ideation (Vintimilla, 2023). This practice helps us to orient and discern within and through the open field of potentiality. Pedagogical ideation aims to activate ideas and create interstices that craft unknown possibilities. These possibilities orient toward and project into what is significant and makes a difference. For us, this is the guiding vector of curriculum making.

Circularity here is more than a concept to apply in the curriculum or to explain what takes place or even to discuss with the children. Valeria takes circularity as the material and conceptual fabric of El Vergel, and it becomes a way of knowing and being in the world. Valeria and the children take the garden's invitation to embed circularity as a cosmology. Perhaps this is an instance of insurgent wisdom (Arias, 2018); that is, when circularity takes over El Vergel, it configures Valeria's intentionality. Composing with circularity brings us back to the garden, which beams with life – seeds, seedlings, plants, water, insects are in constant interaction and movement. We get closer to the mundane and ordinary movements that take place in the garden. We spend long periods of time creating life-clay relationships inspired by circular shapes that are present in the garden. We interact with different creatures and plants, and we pay attention to the simple and convivial everyday rhythms in which we coexist with the garden.

## *Trueque* and Reciprocity

Circularity involves practices of reciprocity inherent in the Andean economy of *trueque* (barter). Trueque, as an Andean economy also mirroring cosmoses' circularity, involves the mutual exchange of goods, labour, or things, which in turn creates a commons among kin. In trueque, one is not a simple consumer or receiver but participates and is co-present in a collective. Trueque is a practice that makes us highly aware that we occupy a space in a broader cosmos of relations and interactions. It highlights not only that we are interdependent but that we are called into keeping a process alive, which, in turn, makes us active participants in an economy and in an axiology that is generated in ritualized customs of trueque.

Although we could easily suggest that Valeria engages in trueque as a way of introducing children to a fixed and idealized past economy, what we want to highlight here is that Valeria brings reciprocity as another mode of relating and thinking. In trueque, "reciprocity is not conceived as a fixed principle with definitive rules but rather as a principle that enables a complex system of relation making between the different identities in the cosmos" (Beauclair, 2013, p. 40, our translation). In El Vergel garden, trueque becomes one of the practices that create an educational space as a meeting place where complex webs of relation are nurtured. In this way, the educational space is not reduced to a space for transmission, regulation, or socialization or even defined only as a space for learning. Rather, we propose the educational space that emerges in this garden as dialogical, relational, and creative. It is a space that requires our presence as much as it requires that we notice our reciprocal obligations and abilities to consider the well-being of many and not only of one. When these obligations are recognized, we engage with an educational space that enables acts of reciprocity within and across multiple forms of commons: "biophysical commons (e.g., soil, water, air, plant, and animal ecologies), cultural commons (e.g., language, musical heritage, sacred symbols, and artworks), social commons (e.g., educational, health, and political systems), and knowledge commons (e.g., Indigenous ecological knowledge, scientific, and technical knowledge)" (Gibson-Graham et al., 2016, p. 195).

When foraging and harvesting, children engage in acts of mutuality and reciprocity: Figs are shared, blackberries are exchanged for *capulies* (a type of Andean cherry), and golden berries are gifted in gratitude for lemons the children received. What matters to Valeria is the potential for reciprocity as a "creative strategy for surviving" (Sammells, 2019, p. 259) among and across commons. Through the multiple trueques, or exchanges, children offer and receive seeds of all kinds, and as if they were inspired to keep up with an established circular rhythm across commons, they decide to plant the seeds in their clay vessels, returning in this way to the containers of life. The seeds and the act of planting germinate a question that still resonates with us: What would the world be if we were seeds? Again, we think here with the concept of proximity, of contact and embodiment, where planting is not enough.

What matters is the affective necessity to become the seed and create stories out of this becoming, producing a relational space that stories new life possibilities and where "many different combinations of fertile existences" appear to be possible (Bourriaud, 2002, p. 46).

In El Vergel, we experienced an educational space invigorated by pedagogies that nourished multidimensional webs of dialogue and speculative imagination emerging from the children's questions and wonderments about the circularity of living and dying. The pedagogies in El Vergel created a proximity with the mystery of these dimensions without presuming solutions or certainties and without following the conventional avoidance of dialogue with children about these existential matters. The attentiveness that characterized the educational space in El Vergel often immersed us in processes outside the frames of meaning (of life or death); nevertheless, it did not fail to compose a world that felt significant, rich, and above all capable of offering possibilities to experience alternative relational logics.

# 4 Multiple Platitudes of Soil, History, and Memory: Cabogana Garden

Figure 4.1. Speculative Drawing: Cabogana Garden

Cabogana mountain is part of the Andean range that embraces the city of Cuenca. To get to Cabogana, we walk roads that rise gradually, revealing complex landscapes full of contrast that form the city's valley. Ancient villages rich in tradition and memories – both natural and cultural – settle on the Cabogana slopes while urban development grows and stifles its traditional rurality. This area of Cuenca is characterized by the many small mountain creeks that intermingle with rich, colourful clay soil. For decades, this soil has been the source for traditional brick and tile making. As you drive through this area, it is impossible to miss the brick and tile kilns spread across the uneven land. The kilns appear intertwined with grocery stores and restaurants providing a mix of traditional and fast food, internet cafes, and one of the city's main shopping centres.

In this chapter, we narrate the pedagogical work and curricular trajectories of Cabogana garden (https://viraltimes.climateactionchildhood.net/index.php/gardens/cabogana-garden/). Alongside the children and Andrea, the teacher, in Cabogana we focus on how proximities with clay bring us closer to the histories and memories embedded in the soil of this mountain. Pedagogically, we engage with processes that open multiple alternative temporalities to recognize soil as a pedagogical protagonist enabling and inviting us to pay attention to coexistences, transformation, and corporality. In turn, these concepts allow us to experiment with generative tensions within pedagogical events, child-clay storying, and collective memory.

## Weakening Capitalist Temporalities

Clay – with its histories, memories, colours, and textures – is the material we come across every day in the Cabogana garden. From the very start of our pedagogical work in Cabogana, clay has been the co-protagonist of our encounters. As we engaged in the pedagogical processes that gave life to Cabogana's educational experiences, clay invited us to think with different temporalities. This invitation openly interrupted an accelerated rhythm that impregnated the pedagogical work in this garden. These rhythms are not hard to recognize. They are the accelerated rhythms of late neoliberal-capitalist production. These rhythms mark – day after day – the pedagogical tempo of so many schools. They are rhythms that create us. We are of them. They organize our corporeal experiences.[1] As Barone Zallocco and Díaz (2023) write: "Under the rhythmic morality of productive time, [capitalist productivity] is not only incited but desired. The velocity of capital is no longer a

1 In the itinerant school we speak of *cuerpos*, which, when translated to *bodies*, loses the more complex and ontological sense that cuerpos affords. Thus, in this case we prefer to translate to corporeal.

rhythm external to our existence but is the favourite tranquilizer of our sensitivity" (p. 35, our translation).

Clay, however, interrupts this productive time and turns our attention toward other temporalities. Clay's sticky constitution touches and sticks to shoes, demanding more attention to balance when walking. It makes us slow down; it brings a different awareness to what is going on when our feet touch the ground. When we touch clay, it permeates; it takes up space in and on every part of our bodies: hands, feet, hair, arms, etc. Clay is not easily contained. Its colours enchant us. It's impossible not to stop, not to stay there mesmerized at times, noticing, feeling, and slowing down. In this slowing down, we notice details that – otherwise – would have been hard to notice. Experiencing these other rhythms is not easy. As Barone Zallocco and Díaz (2021) point out, if life does not move "at a pace of multidimensional, multitasking connectivity, we surely find a feeling of boredom or evident drowsiness" (p. 29, our translation). We certainly face similar moments with the children when trying to slow down – when trying to find other processes and rhythms that might help us notice how implicated we are in what we are noticing (Jardine, 2008). In these moments, we ask ourselves how we might stay faithful to these other pedagogical rhythms, how we might find momentum that is not based on "capital flows that set the pace of normalized life" (Barone Zallocco & Díaz, p. 35, our translation).

Clay compels us to find other fluxes, to slow down processes, find what before was unnoticeable yet abundantly present – in front of and around us. In this garden, we learn to notice differently. For us, this difference comes from "whiling" (Jardine, 2008, p. 3). David Jardine (2008) says that whiling, or worthwhileness,

> has to do with a way of treating things, a way of composing our understanding of something, seeking its kinships (Wittgenstein 1968, 36) and verisimilitudes (Gadamer 1989, 21), and, in the same breath, composing ourselves, finding our composure in the face of what we have encountered. (p. 5)

In this, our work finds a pedagogical vitality that we believe would have been impossible had we stayed in the efficient – yet stagnating and normative – rhythms with which we started the work in Cabogana.

## Relational Attention

In Cabogana, as in other gardens, our proximity with clay becomes an experience of coexistence that is not based on establishing mastery or acquiring knowledge. Knowledge, with its thirst for certainty and predictability, makes us turn our back to the world (Ingold, 2022a). Instead, Cabogana, with its proximity to and encounters with clay, is an inviting coexistence towards enhancing relational attention to other logics and languages and to articulating stories that emerge within this relational attention. This is an attention that, for us, holds powerful pedagogical implications as it makes evident that the language of relations is never monolinguistic and that, in these proximities, our identities transform and extend (Glissant, 1997). In the itinerant school, this relational attention and its pedagogical implication help us keep alive the multiform nature of education and to avoid reducing it to uniform processes of mere instruction and application.

Moist, sticky, soft lumps of clay meet the dryness of hands and begin to mould themselves on contact, finding a new shape. As time passes, the children and Andrea, the teacher, are fascinated by animating and enlivening encounters with water, bodies, and clay soil. We create a collective conversation about emerging shapes and colours and the giving form and deforming that happen between wet clay and children. In being with clay, children become curious and attentive to clay's transformative force. On being with the world and things, Ingold (2022a) writes: "in allowing ourselves into their presence rather than holding them at arm's length – in attending to them – we find that they are also guiding our attention" (p. 23). In attending to clay's presence in Cabogana, the children and Andrea are fascinated by how, as clay shifts, morphs, permeates, and transforms, they too are transformed.

## Animated Clay-Child Proximities

Clay with its earthiness opens the possibility for novel ways to think about relations and about becoming. In proximity with clay, in the middle of its stickiness to bodies, its shifting forms, and children's transforming perceptions, we see – following Manning (2020) – that the becoming-child is subjectively reoriented: "to become," Manning writes, "is to be reoriented by the germs of existence in formation" (p. 7), and as we experience in Cabogana, to become is also to give life to otherwise relational logics:

> Subjects are born of the occasion, affected, and affecting within the matrix of its singular conditions of existence. There is no mediation here: the subject cannot be passed, externalized, abstracted from the occasion. Body-worlds are a constellation. (Manning, 2020, p. 2)

With Manning's proposition, we may consider proximities with clay soil as creating a pedagogical occasion that enables intimate and collective inquiries, ones that reorient and challenge sovereign human delimitations. These delimitations position humans above and apart from the world. Our encounters with clay challenge the separation that conceives soil as inert matter to be used and exploited by humans.

The pedagogical processes we put in motion in Cabogana trouble what Barone Zallocco and Díaz (2021) call "oppressive modes of limits ... that operate as a fence of impediments" (p. 34, our translation). In education, this "fence of impediments" impedes webs of relations – webs that have the potential to create educational experiences that intimately involve us with the world and where interdependence is intensified. In Cabogana, pedagogical encounters that create conditions for such intimacy are organized and staged by affirming and attending to the entanglements emerging in child-clay proximities. We do this while fully realizing that doing pedagogies that try to challenge the limits of human supremacy – and its alliances with capitalism – is easier said than done. Such pedagogies require a pedagogical praxis that does not dismay in the face of emerging resistances, impasses, and even the aporias that appear when trying to distance from obstinate traditional instructional habits of achieving curricular objectives, giving explanations, and evaluating facts and content accumulation as a guarantee of knowledge. This is a praxis in pedagogical wilfulness and defiance that enables us to affirm different sensitivities "that truly bind us to the world, that world of plural existence that we are tracing in these wanderings" (Barone Zallocco & Díaz, 2021, p. 34). We speak here of sensitivities because this praxis does not produce new identities but rather a different way to tend to things, a "tendency" (Manning, 2020) that has the potential to "make different."

In the encounters of children's bodies, clay, and water there is a fluidity, an expansive permeability, that is unavoidable. Wet Cabogana clay does not stay contained. It relates, it spills out, it impregnates: leaves, rocks, hands, and feet. Provoked by this uncontainability and keeping close to Manning's ideas, we insist that our pedagogical work rethink our ideas on bodies as contained, individual, and enclosed. In this insistence, we take inspiration from the work of many Latin American feminist, antiracist, and decolonial thinkers and activists (Glockner et al., 2023; Zaragocin & Caretta, 2020) who have introduced the concept of *cuerpo-territorio* to highlight an approach to the body and land as expressing and "stemming from the collective history, culture, and spirituality of peoples and individuals who created and belong to such ancestral lands" (Glockner et al., 2023, p. 7). We think with cuerpo-territorio to complexify our reference to the English word *bodies*, and we think of them not as simply contained and individual but rather "shared in communal, cultural, spiritual, and familial ties" (p. 7). In this way, we are reminded that the proximities and coexistences happening in this garden are not isolated and cannot be indifferent to those happening beyond the garden's limits. We work hard to think about these encounters without being oblivious to historically longstanding and multigenerational cuerpo-territorio relations that make the everyday life of this neighbourhood in the city.

## Clay's Alphabet

Cabogana's clay – with its multiplicity of textures and colours – is materially made of the relations with *territorio* and, at the same time, it is the co-maker of the longstanding histories and stories that shape this neighbourhood. As days go by, the children and Andrea correspond with clay. In these exchanges, stories emerge. These are stories where authorship is shared and "penned down" in the middle space of encounters among children, teacher, and clay. This is a space we attend and pedagogically compose. We do this without wanting to control or deprive it of its indefiniteness and indiscernibility. Rather, we attempt to attune and pedagogically speculate on the basis of its possible and generative unfolding. In other words, as we mentioned before, the proximity with clay is not based on a pedagogical logic driven by the desire to teach, to explain, to make meaning, or even to represent. Following Stengers (2017), we could say that pedagogical speculation aims "at maximising friction with experience, refusing the right every specialised thought grants itself: to explain, while eliminating anything that cannot be framed by the explanation" (p. 16). In this, we support our interest in Cabogana to refuse a reductive understanding of pedagogical work as translated into mere explanation (i.e., teachers explaining to children what they don't know).

In this maximizing and refusal, a vitality emerges as the children and Andrea notice clay's language of transformation, flexibility, movement, symbiosis, and variety. They recognize fullness and plurality in clay's language. In these rich and vibrant correspondences with clay, an alphabet of clay is slowly created (see alphabet here: https://viraltimes.climateactionchildhood.net/index.php/gardens/cabogana-garden/clay-alphabet/). As Andrea spends time with the children, we carefully notice the ways in which this alphabet is conceived and takes form. We realize that the alphabet is not created to linguistically represent something but to entangle ourselves even more with the logics of clay and collectively produce stories. These are child-clay stories that stick to our imagination and awaken our interest in the stories that make this place and are beyond the garden walls – just as if child-clay stories slowly percolate through the garden limits searching for other cuerpo-territorio stories.

It would not be unusual, at this point, to succumb to the educational anxieties that would require we ignore clay's alphabet and instead efficiently teach the conventional alphabet that visually represents verbal communication and is a key foundational element in children's reading and writing, the alphabet that in modern schooling is considered indispensable and important knowledge. Our intention is not to dismiss this relevancy; however, in our work in Cabogana, we question its centrality in literacy processes. Following the pedagogical wilfulness mentioned earlier, we decide to preserve and create with the alphabet that this experience makes important (Stengers, 2017). As Stengers writes: "importance can never be reduced to a de facto or given situation" (p. 17); making something important (a situation, an object, an alphabet) "means intensifying the sense of possibles that it harbours, as expressed by the struggles and claims to another way of making it exist" (p. 17). We work with and through the struggles of legitimization that this alphabet provokes. At the same time, "harbouring possibilities" keep emerging.

As the children and Andrea continue enlivening the alphabet by noticing clay's specificities and its dynamic transformations, clay slowly dries, crumbles, and becomes coloured powder. A variety of clay colours (terra cotta, yellows, white, grey, red, pink) and their textures become the enablers of fabulations and imaginative speculations. Colours have the agency to story, sometimes short-lived stories and other times elaborate ones. The alphabet morphologizes into an alphabet of colours that challenges the limits of representation while also delving into children's personal experiences. For instance, a white silvery colour is named cocoa colour, or a pale yellow colour is named "blueberry ring colour." To these colours, in an almost poetical move, the children assign textures and flavours: pink colour has a "soft papery texture" and "watermelon flavour" while *florcita* (little flower) colour has a "soft and hard texture" and a "strawberry flavour." The alphabet of colours does not work as an object or system of classification. Rather, each colour gradience stories distinct worlds. The pink colour tells the story of the universe where the "universe bathes in a sea of light" that is seen and unseen, ancient and new. Other colours tell interwoven stories of humans and animals and others of memory and footprints. In this, we think about colours as a perceptive phenomenon that is at the same time a cultural and affective creation in which we participate. These stories become the eventful force for collective storytelling and pedagogical micro-experimentations in reading and writing. What we find in these pedagogical and aesthetic experiences is literacy feeling vital (Snaza, 2021) and becoming an "animate practice" (Snaza, 2019, p. 4), which, in turn, challenges traditional understandings of literacy as a representational practice of children's meaning making "where knowing subjects make sense of objects functioning as media" (Snaza, 2021, p. 254) and thus miss "everything about literacy that is vital" (p. 254).

The vital literacies we experienced in Cabogana indicate a vitality that is not intrinsic to the self-contained child or their meaning making, nor to the colours of clay – in itself – but to what went on and was activated in the compositional space of this pedagogical event. Here, literacy "is primarily about effects and not conscious events of meaning making or representational constructions" (Snaza, 2019, p. 17). Inspired by Nathan Snaza's writing on Gail Boldt's ideas on vitality, we could say that pedagogical vitality "is produced and keeps things in motion; it does not belong to any of the elements but is the energy that flows through the elements, belonging to the event" (Boldt, as cited in Snaza, 2021, p. 254). In other words, for us, pedagogical work creatively and interpretively attends to what is produced and energized within curricular processes and among the elements of a situated pedagogical context. It does this without falling into a kind of presentism or ahistorical vacuum. Pedagogical work is embedded in the often difficult process of historically inheriting while – through those very curricular processes – producing artifacts of collective memory. Here, we are insisting on an idea of education as what implicates us and calls us to respond to a specific inheritance – its history and present – in which we participate.

In Cabogana, we experience this double movement when the work with the alphabet of colours brings us closer to an old, unused brick and tile kiln that is part of the garden. The kiln is an artifact packed with family affect and stories. At the same time, it is an artifact connected to a broader legacy of this place, one that reflects the artisanal and socioeconomic unevenness that makes this Andean city. The pedagogical processes we enacted gesture towards what di Paoloantonio (2023) refers to as *passing on*. Education, he writes, "helps us to 'pass on', welcoming what is beyond me, inheriting from the past for the sake of 'what is to come'" (p. 112). The children and Andrea collectively attend to the legacies the kiln evokes. Multiple stories emerge in these encounters and propelled them to go outside the garden walls to meet Rosita and her family's legacy as brick makers. We see the kiln as an artifact that "renders legible the borders of a certain inheritance" (di Paoloantonio, 2023, p. 119) and creates, even if in imperfect ways, a proximity to our collective "owed responsibility" (p. 119) toward an inheritance that carries stories of beauty and sorrow, of extraction and creation or artistry and struggle.

With the kiln, Andrea and the children rearrange static understandings of the relation past-future and reconfigure their relation with the old and new. As di Paoloantonio (2023) writes,

> by infusing the continuously receding and fragmentary heritage from the past with our own unique temporal perspective, we create something new and distinctive that adds to an enduring legacy and sensibility, capable of being meaningfully passed on to future generations who themselves are bestowed with a turn at bringing something new to the world. (p. 110)

We end our work in Cabogana carrying with us, once again, a deep acknowledgment that the flow of pedagogical energy is future oriented – thus we are always envisioning ways that might allow us to create educational experiences where we can keep the future alive.

# 5 Encountering Chickens' Singularities: El Tejar Garden

Figure 5.1. Speculative Drawing: El Tejar Garden

Unlike the itinerant school's other gardens in urban backyards, El Tejar (https://viraltimes.climateactionchildhood.net/index.php/gardens/el-tejar-garden/) is located on a sizable piece of vacant land belonging to the father of the teacher, Karina. Karina's father acquired the land for his civil engineering company. He eventually built a warehouse for storing his company's materials and machinery, first consisting of a covered patio with four corner posts and a zinc roof; he later built walls using available recycled materials. This modest construction then became a full-time house for a rural migrant employee and his family.

At the time the itinerant school opened, the house was vacant. The children spent their school days outdoors and used the dining room as a gathering space at the end of each day.

A second building on the property is a sophisticated chicken coop with nesting boxes, roosting bars, space for a feeder and waterer, and vents for air circulation. Originally, the coop housed two hens and a rooster; the first hen unexpectedly arrived on the land and quickly became a permanent resident; the second was a gift to Karina's father from a neighbour and was meant to be eaten. Unable to kill the hen, Karina's father bought a rooster for breeding. Now, between hens and roosters, a flock of about fifteen birds roams freely around the vacant property. Karina's father feeds the chickens daily and collects the many eggs the hens leave scattered around the land.

Thus, El Tejar is not an ordinary educational space. Children and a large flock of avians share and negotiate (not always successfully) this space in the Cabogana neighbourhood. The presence of chickens in early childhood spaces is not unusual. We often read that introducing chickens into classrooms holds significant educational value through fostering a unique and interactive learning environment – chickens might serve as living, breathing lessons in responsibility, empathy, and compassion as children witness the needs and emotions of these creatures; children might gain hands-on experience in caring for these feathered animals, learning about their life cycle, animal behaviour, and the importance of nutrition; further, observing chickens' daily routines might provide a tangible connection to sustainability as children comprehend the origins of food and the environmental impacts of agriculture.

## Being and Doing with a Flock of Chickens

Overall, in the literature, the presence of chickens in classrooms enriches education by offering practical, real-world applications that instill in children a sense of stewardship and a deeper understanding of the natural world (Purewal et al., 2017; Wolff et al., 2018). Yet, in El Tejar, these are not topics of conversations among the children and the teacher, the children themselves, nor the teacher and us. And this is not only because El Tejar's hens and roosters live in the wild (as opposed to being caged in a classroom) but because we conceptualize the pedagogical encounters nurtured here in opposition to the notion that chickens exist in the world for human benefit. The presence of a flock of chickens plays a key role in configuring the garden; what matters is that these creatures live an active existence.

The conversations and daily engagements in El Tejar provide a space for thinking alternatives to human-centred pedagogy that supports the "current individualistic culture" and maintains the modern nature/culture divide (Mustola, 2019, p. 1435). In El Tejar, the notion of the modern human is in question. Tsing (2020) explains:

> Bringing living beings into the redefinition of the human comes from animal studies, where ethical questions have helped to reframe the relation between humans and nonhumans. If we learn to imagine animals not as a class of deferent or pesky others, but rather as individuals with whom we can develop a relation of mutual response, we might open our social lives beyond the human as we knew it. (p. 3)

A way of developing such a relation of mutual response and challenging the conscious, intentional, rational, and masterful human is by working with children to expand notions of agency, crossing species boundaries, that is, looking "at non-humans as active beings and historical actors that shape the worlds that both they and other species – including humans – live in" (Hathaway, 2015, p. 240). We invite children to notice the feathered creatures they share a space with as world-making actors and to see themselves as "co-participants with non-human species, imagining new worlds that eschew anthropocentrism" (Hathaway, p. 240; also see Potts, 2012). Children notice that the hens and roosters don't just live in the garden but create what the garden has become: a world with holes in the ground, hiding spots, spaces for laying eggs, sounds that fill the space, and so on.

Inspired by the scholarship of feminist philosopher Donna Haraway, we work to create possibilities for chickens and children to encounter each other as companion species. As Haraway and chicken advocate Annie Potts explain,

> the concept of companion species plays the cat's cradle games where who is/are to be in the world gets constituted in intra- and inter-action. The partners do not precede the meeting; species of all kinds are consequent upon subject- and object-shaping entanglements. In human-animal worlds, companion species are ordinary beings in-encounter in the house, lab, field, zoo, park, truck, office, prison, ranch, arena, village, human hospital, slaughter house, vet clinic, stadium, barn, wildlife preserve, farm, city streets, factory, and more. (Potts & Haraway, 2010, p. 322)

This companion species relation "involves not just knowing but also doing" (Rose & van Dooren, 2021, p. 35). This doing includes what Rose and van Dooren (2021) describe as "a kind of response – grounded in close attention – that takes an interest in what matters to another rather than reading one's own positioning onto them" (p. 35). We notice that children are captivated by chickens' movements, and some of the birds respond to children's curiosities by coming close. Thus, we open up a space for creative ways of "walking" together. The children imagine what it would be like to walk like chickens do, using sticks that mimic a chicken's leg, and through drawing. Drawing is a medium that allows the children to pay close attention to these avians' particular movements. We cannot say that the children have learned to walk like hens or roosters as they struggle to meet the speed at which chickens walk. For us, however, it is not about children getting the movement right. We agree with Rose and van Dooren that "what is at stake here is learning how to better see and understand the lively responsiveness of our world" (p. 33) in order for children to nurture more liveable ways of responding to the more-than-human. As children and chickens encounter each other in the garden, they are "in knots of becoming with each other that shape worlds and ways of [possibly] nurturing other sorts of liveable worlds" (Potts & Haraway, 2010, p. 324). We articulate educational processes that address these "knots of becoming." These articulations engage us in a dynamic exchange with Karina as we delve into her perspectives on education, which intertwine with the alternative notions of relationality taking shape in this context.

## Noticing Avian Singularities

In addition to bringing the agency of hens and roosters to the forefront, we attend to the singularities of these feathered beings, emphasizing their vitality. Rather than learning about these birds, children engage in learning with them. Despret (2008), a Belgian philosopher and ethologist, provides a nuanced perspective to the understanding of animals by challenging the traditional scientific approach that tends to reduce animals to mere objects of study. Instead, she proposes that animals actively shape their own behaviours and experiences. Certainly, this is not an easy pedagogical move. For weeks, Karina struggles to engage in practices that gesture towards learning with chickens. It takes time and intentional pedagogical effort for children in El Tejar to begin to recognize each hen and rooster as a sentient being with subjectivity. Attending to the complexities of human-animal relationships, the children move away from generic conceptualizations of "chickens" as they relate to each creature in their singularity: the fearful hen, the rooster that eats all day, the rooster with the large crest, the injured rooster, the hen with the tousled feathers, the old hen that spends much of her time laying down, the hen that makes a sound when eating, the mother hen, and so on.

This deeply relational engagement that children create with hens and roosters extends toward an experimentation with interspecies communication. Despret (2015, 2016) suggests that communication across species boundaries is a complex and reciprocal process that demands a willingness to listen and acknowledge the diverse forms of expression found in animals' worlds. Children think about the ways these unique beings engage with and interpret the world. They spend weeks attending to the symbiosis between the rooster and a grain of corn. They notice how the rooster enthusiastically pecks at the scattered corn kernels, using his beak to pick up an individual grain while scratching the ground with his foot. By recognizing the richness of these actions, the children experiment with and invent ways to communicate with the rooster (having to think beyond humancentric notions of communication). As we explained in Chapter 2, we frame these acts of communication as an existential form of reaching out, of noticing each other's presences rather than an exchange to gain knowledge.

As the documentation for El Tejar garden shows, children's attempts to communicate with the chickens are not always successful (https://viraltimes.climateactionchildhood.net/index.php/gardens/el-tejar-garden/). Yet, pedagogically, what matters is the difficulties that emerge in children's attempts to encounter the irreconcilable differences and their deep desire to engage the other without making it the same (Todd, 2023). Shifts within and continuities between notions of self and other emerge in the midst of curriculum making. Children grapple with notions of existence and relating as they embrace the puzzlements that emerge from the incommensurabilities between their own and their avian companions' lives. Importantly, they do this difficult work through tangible real-life connections and experiences – in Haraway's words, through "relationships in the flesh" (Potts & Haraway, 2010, p. 320).

## Acts of Worlding with Hens and Eggs

Children's curiosity extends beyond chickens' singularities. Children are fascinated by how hens care for the eggs and by what might lie within an egg. As they encounter the eggs throughout the property, children envision the myriad possibilities of life dwelling within these eggs. The mere thought of inhabiting an egg sparks a cascade of speculative conjectures, prompting them to ponder the sensations of warmth and snugness that such a confined space might offer. In this speculative journey, the inside of an egg becomes a cozy sanctuary, a secret world where magical creatures or fantastical scenarios unfold, as well as a space to wonder about daily life difficulties. We might readily interpret these as moments for children to explore their innocent curiosity and/or to nurture their imaginative ideas and/or even as a way to understand the wonders of life and the limitless potential that lies beyond the ordinary. Yet, for us, these acts are pedagogical and not merely cognitively beneficial for children's development. To address what we mean by these acts being pedagogical, we draw on the environmental humanities and educational theorists who think with this emerging field.

Inviting children to experiment with modes of communicating with these hens and to think about the inside of the egg involves "effort to open up space for the multiplication of creative forms of attention toward other-than-human modes of worlding" (van Dooren, 2019, p. 18). We are attempting to respond to children's predicaments around the hens and the eggs by activating, as education philosopher Todd (2023, p. 2) says, the idea of "worlding" in our pedagogical practice. Worlding, Todd tells us, means "the ways in which the world is brought into being at the same time as one is brought into being with it" (p. 2): the "co-constitution of worlds and human subjects" simultaneously (p. 3). Worlding, Todd emphasizes, "can bring into being and make present a world through our interconnection with it" and "through its sensory engagement in the present" (p. 2). She calls these pedagogies of worlding and cautions that "worlding is less about having students recognize their relation to the world, as though the world were separate from them, and more about engaging students in their already existing relations of the world with which they are entwined" (p. 3).

For Todd (2023), the role of the sensorial is key in worlding pedagogies because it is through the senses that children connect and feel part of a world in intimate and concrete ways. It is worth quoting Todd at length here:

> Through aesthetic worlding practices, two things happen: First, a child becomes *part of* their environment – social, cultural, biological – in ways, importantly, that are not simply *determined* by that environment. That is, through their encounters, they feel their way through what is given [hens and eggs, for example] and bring their own histories, languages, cultural practices to these unique encounters that defy any specific predetermined outcome. Secondly, it is precisely the unpredictability of touching, smelling, hearing or tasting something that enables children to become with

> the world in each their own way. There is thus something both shared and common, on the one hand, and singular and unique, on the other. (p. 12, emphasis in original)

In El Tejar, when Karina invites the children to become the inside of an egg using creative bodily engagements, to transform themselves into the hen to get closer to the chicks, and to speculate making nests for the hens to lay their eggs, different modes of becoming with the more-than-human are being made possible. In other words, the interwoven semiotic and material trajectories of children and chickens are constitutive of and reconstituted by their encounters. Children become implicated in worlds, with all their vulnerabilities. For these children, there is not a world out there to be managed in specific ways by them alone. Rather, they are materially and semiotically engaged with the more-than-human in processes of co-creation, co-generation, co-emergence and making worlds together – a world that cannot be simply ordered in ways that are advantageous for children. This is akin to what Common World Research Collective's researchers have referred to as pedagogies that decentre the child by attending to the relational and collective agency of/within the world (Taylor & Pacini-Ketchabaw, 2017, 2018). For us, in the itinerant school, these interwoven trajectories are charged with a desire to propose an education that troubles the modern idea that the only "real" educator is man and that humans can only learn from other humans or that only humans are worthy of education because education is what humanizes and thus placing the autonomous human above all other species. This category of man has dominated the educational imaginary for centuries, making almost impossible an idea of pedagogy and educational praxis configured in an alternative onto-epistemology, one that will also enable us, among other things, to deeply rethink schooling or, to say it with Duschatzky (2005; also Duschatzky & Aguirre, 2019), to disassemble schooling.

## Life-Death Approximations

As in El Vergel (Chapter 3), children in El Tejar encounter life's circularity. A few days after the excitement of encountering a hen being followed by a large flock of young chicks, the unexpected, surprising, and disarming event of a dying chick brings children to witness the vulnerability of life. As they stumble upon the fragile body of the chick in its final moments, a tumultuous wave of mixed affects envelops them. The children delicately care for the creature and engage in a profound contemplation around the ephemeral nature of existence. As Valeria (the teacher in Chapter 3), Karina, and the children accompany the dying/dead chick by providing spaces for care, mourning, ceremony, and ritual, they (consciously or unconsciously) reconfigure dominant notions of school.

Duschatzky (2005; also Duschatzky & Aguirre, 2019) might call this reconfiguration *des-armando escuela* (disassembling school), proposing that instead of arranging the school as a space for "forging its inhabitants" we think it as "a space taken over by heterogeneous presences that can be thought of in multiple and contingent configurations" (2005, p. 79). In other words, the school is made by the multiple presences that take it over, and the question becomes what we might do/how we might relate to what emerges in the midst of our lives. These are spaces, Duschatzky and Aguirre (2019) suggest, that are felt, thought through, fully inhabited, and passionately discussed rather than spaces where rehearsed responses are applied. When we approach educational spaces this way, Duschatzky writes, "it is not then a question of an educational experience, but of an experience that happens in an educational space" (2005, p. 79).

The dying/dead chick does not represent an experience that allows children to learn about death. The event becomes a problem but not a problem to be solved. This is a problem that gathers children and teachers in El Vergel and El Tejar, inviting them to take part in an event in which many things might happen. It is an event in which children experience the challenge of dying. Said differently, the dying chick does not become a problem for the gardens; rather, the gardens are put into question by the event. Duschatzky (2005) suggests that the event itself challenges the limits of what a school is allowed to be and what a school is allowed to think. While traditionally a school is a space that separates children from what we don't yet know how to think, the gardens in the itinerant school are connective nodes to think "the field of the possible and not of what is necessary" (p. 82). In Duschatzky's words, "it is necessary if it is reducible to a correspondence with a state of affairs; it's possible if a movement of thought brings the potential into existence (2005, p. 82). In these gardens, then, the unfortunate event of the dying chick generates intense affects that summon children and teachers to think what might be possible.

In El Tejar, we invented pedagogical processes alongside curricular trajectories to respond to a particular place and its inhabitants – the chickens that roam the garden became key protagonists as children engaged in thinking and rethinking important ontological questions pertaining to modes of being and becoming in a complex world. This was an educational space that refused the notion of the anthropos as ideal. Through this refusal, El Tejar welcomed problems and invited the possibility of altered subjectivities. Children were not necessarily socialized into an existing world. Instead, we beckoned to children to be moved by and to respond to an unexpected and unpredictable world without models or guarantees. This does not mean that El Tejar was an educational space without a trajectory. It means, instead, that El Tejar was an educational space without a predetermined trajectory for already-known forms of subjectivity.

# 6 Soil as Life, Life as Soil: Composting Pedagogies in Naranay Garden

WITH ALICJA FRANKOWSKI

Figure 6.1. Speculative Drawing: Narancay Garden

In the aftermath of the devastating loss of the magnificent vegetable gardens referred to by locals as *los jardines de Narancay*, a new community has emerged. The once lush greenery has been replaced with state-of-the-art infrastructure, modern buildings, and busy streets lined with shops and businesses. While many in the city reminisce about the beauty of this area, a group of children in the itinerant school discusses the remnants concealed beneath the layers of soil where those gardens once adorned the neighbourhood. In Narancay, the children are fascinated by the histories that are composting and mixing with Andean volcanic stardust beneath the commercial hub. Ximena, the teacher, joins the children as they ponder the composition of this soil, its inhabitants, and its care. From here, educational possibilities unfold in a house garden abandoned due to urbanization. In this chapter, we narrate the composting pedagogies we nurtured in Narancay garden and traced in the pedagogical documentation we created (https://viraltimes.climateactionchildhood.net/index.php/gardens/narancay-eng/).

## Composting Pedagogies

As we attune to the presences in this garden and begin doing composting pedagogies, the work of feminist philosophers Haraway (2016) and Puig de la Bellacasa (2015, 2019) offers provoking and generative companionship. We generate conditions for collective communities of multispecies to flourish. Pedagogically, composting in Narancay involves processes of relearning "how to conjugate worlds with partial connections" across species (Haraway, 2016, p. 13). Haraway's concept of composting complexifies our pedagogical thinking about the processes and trajectories in Narancay. That is not to say that pedagogies of composting show how children learn to compost. It is correct that the children gesture toward practices of composting in the garden. Children find scraps of fruits and observe as these slowly return to the soil through decomposition. However, what matters, for us, is how to work with the pedagogical potential that composting offers – put differently, to attempt to pedagogically nurture, lean towards, learn, and think with practices of composting. This matters because, in conjugating alternative worlds, and more specifically, for us, educational worlds, we seek a pedagogical vitality that surpasses the standardized continuity through which we conduct educational practices. We seek conditions for relearning understood as re-existing because these conditions enable us to rethink what is going on, who we are, and how we are becoming (Barone Zallocco & Díaz, 2023). Composting pedagogies are pedagogies infused in the vitality intrinsic in existential processes of composing, decomposing, and co-composing.

What is involved in composting pedagogies? With Haraway (2016), we attend to compostists' practices:

> Compostists [not only find] out everything they [can] about experimental, intentional, utopian, dystopian, and revolutionary communities and

> movements across times and places. One of their great disappointments in these accounts [is beginning] from the premises of starting over and beginning anew, instead of learning to inherit without denial and stay with the trouble of damaged worlds. Although hardly free of the sterilizing narrative of wiping the world clean by apocalypse or salvation, the richest humus for their inquiries turned out to be sf – science fiction and fantasy, speculative fabulation, speculative feminism, and string figures. Blocking the foreclosures of utopias, sf kept politics alive. (p. 150)

Haraway points us towards the idea of carefully inheriting what comes to the compost bin, carefully attending, that is, to the narratives and logics that teem with life in Narancay garden so that we can attempt to approximate alternative ones. As the documentation shows, Ximena, the children, and we work to decompose the dominant narratives over and over again, ensuring that we don't simply attempt to wipe our pedagogies and curriculum trajectories free of problems and questions. Here we are deeply inspired by Barone Zallocco and Díaz (2023) when they refer to similar efforts as a vitalism that resides in the very problems and questions "that avoid immediate and instrumental answers because this would imply a cancellation of movement and the ceaseless choreography of inquiry. These are questions that seize our delayed thinking, making their way with a different force, one that is more rooted in the sensations that compose us" (p. 13, our translation) and where the "few answers we obtain do not command or order, but they do orient us" (p. 14, our translation).

## Decomposition of Modern Narratives and Logics

Multiple modern narratives and logics emerge, as is the case in other gardens, some early on as soon as the children find holes in the soil and others later, when children are up to their elbows in the soil. We might say that the first decomposition happens in the hands of Ximena and the children. They hesitate to touch the soil with their hands, even to consider that thinking with soil might have pedagogical potential. We encounter a prevailing notion of soil as inherently unclean. Some children comment on the presence of germs in the dirt, which is quickly compared to the COVID-19 virus. It is not only the children who are initially unable to be in proximity with soil. Ximena also expresses hesitation to touch and play with the nearby soil. At a time when touch has become risky, even dangerous, the group is cautious about disease. The need to preserve immunologically pure selves becomes a priority.

It is impossible to pinpoint the exact moment this narrative decomposes. Perhaps it is the soil itself that keeps calling the children, or the many creatures that incite the children to get closer and closer, intensifying their imaginative stories. Or perhaps the repeating discussions we and Ximena have about how the pandemic shows us that we are not insular beings. Bodies and their immunologic systems coexist and are *open, exposed* to others, even made in relations with others. We are, as Haraway (2005) reminds us, multirelational and plural. As Haraway explains, immune system cells in our bodies are many, as they are constantly assembling and reassembling and rely on proteins and macromolecules derived through complex processes from entities such as soil – soil that is organized and altered by human bodies. This reassembly is further complexified as both soil and human bodies adapt, sometimes catastrophically, with each other's makeup of bacteria and other microbes upon touch and consumption (by both human and soil).

There is an insistence that exists in the proximity to the ground. This insistence emerges for us in the realization that our feet are intimately connected to soil, ground, and earth. It literally sustains us. This proximity occurs in the constant touch of our feet on the surface, even when this touch is mediated by shoes. We are on it. We are on soil; we are beings together with soil. Even in the midst of the hesitation the children feel, soil's proximity is unavoidable and seductive, hard to resist. Children's bodies bend down as they place the tip of one finger onto the soil. Some children venture to place more than one finger; some place dirt on their hand. Touch brings proximity and articulates unexpected affective responses.

Another modern narrative that composting pedagogies struggle to decompose is the persistent notion that there is no life beyond the human. The challenge at Narancay is to care for soil as living, mysterious, and evocative. It takes careful pedagogical moves to think of soils as being in collaboration with decomposers, to think of worms and bacteria as regenerators of life. Puig de la Bellacasa (2015, 2019) advocates for soil's resurgence, by considering it not just as an inert substrate but as a lively and dynamic entity that embodies care relationships. For Bellacasa, care relationships with soil are speculative efforts that bring us closer to soil and acknowledge our relationalities with it. To experiment with care practices with the soil, we attempt a shift in thinking, from thinking of bacteria in soil as separate from humans, to thinking with relations such as food decaying and returning to soil. Through aesthetic experimentations, we gesture towards soil as not merely a passive resource for exploitation but rather a complex assemblage of living beings, organic matter, and geological formations that sustain life and require attention. Together with Ximena we ask, "How do we care for soil when understanding it as part of us while also being unknowable to us?" How can we approach soil with care, as Bellacasa suggests?

These questions provoke multiple conversations for decomposing traditional schooling approaches towards soil and reevaluating linear and normative conceptions of education driven by educational predictability, learning goals, and standardization. With Ximena, we discuss how we might avoid approaching children's proximity to soil as more than a "learning moment" or as activities that address aspects of the science curriculum. Decomposing these scientific narratives means, for example, that the intricate tunnel designs the children build, including their mysteries and complex interconnected paths, become metaphors for thinking soil's life. Ximena strives to enhance the presence of the soil in the Narancay garden, decomposing narratives that limit soil life to scientific observation pressed onto the group's prior experiences. The questions we work with also open possibilities for teaching differently. Decomposing some of the normative codes of traditional schooling creates a space for teaching to be liberated from compliance or from unquestionably following curriculum coordinates. As in the other gardens, in Narancay we are able to think of pedagogical possibilities that feel more open and stimulating.

Finally, we think with composting pedagogies to decompose capitalist and neoliberal narratives that keep wiggling into the children's storytelling. For instance, children imagine homes underneath the ground as a way of trying to understand worm life, yet representations of private property, home ownership, domestic scenes, and normative family life flood the stories. At times, children's imaginations enforce a life on worms that is stagnant and easily taken away. As a way to decompose these logics and hold onto the vibrancy and multiple presences that make up soil life, we work with children to visualize creatures' bodies differently. We take inspiration from the insects that surface on the grass, such as worms, ants, spiders, scorpions, beetles, and centipedes, and draw our ideas of their bodies. The children sketch out each insect body as an oval or a circle and use coloured pencils and charcoal to design details on them. Finally, we cover the sketches with watercolours. As children continue these powerfully suggestive drawings and paintings, in time, these two-dimensional creatures become three-dimensional as the children create worms out of clay and add them to the soil mixture. Through these practices, dynamics and intensities shift as children become intrigued about coexistence and worms' lifeworlds; they wonder how they and the worms might live with each other and what kinds of habitats worms might prefer. In these wonderings and imaginative moments, we notice not only the children's interest in the lives of worms but perhaps more relevantly a *crossing of worlds*: that of the children and that of the worms and the underneath world of the soil.

The decomposition of these persistent modern narratives and logics is not meant to serve as a way to master knowledge but, as Neimanis and McLauchlan (2022) suggest and as we noted in other chapters, "as a way of co-worlding new and latent possibilities with others" (p. 219) . Furthermore, this co-worlding is not an attempt at signification or meaning making (nor an absence of it); rather, it emphasizes plural interdependency. As Nancy (2000) reminds us, being can only be a being-together. This then means that composting involves more than decomposition (more than being taken apart); it also involves creation. Composting "grows new worlds by putting what is already at hand into careful relation with whatever else shows up" (p. 221). To this end, the decomposition practices we speak of above also "enrich the soil," the inquiry itself, children's lifeworlds, and Ximena's practices (Neimanis & McLauchlan, 2022, p. 221). Moreover, as the pedagogical documentation shows, composting pedagogies also involve adding "nutrition and energy" into the "compost mix" (p. 221). We might say that in Narancay, proximity to soil and its inhabitants is carefully nourished by slowing down, by relational caring practices, and by speculative storytelling.

## Composting Pedagogies Require Time

Akin to Haraway's (2016) composting practices, composting pedagogies need time. Not capitalist notions of time driven by humans' need to control but "the temporal rhythms of more than human worlds" (Puig de la Bellacasa, 2015, p. 695), or, as Puig de la Bellacasa (2017) calls them, "the times of soil" (p. 201). In this way, as we have written elsewhere (Vintimilla & Pacini-Ketchabaw, 2020), composting pedagogies require making time for sensorial/aesthetic encounters; they deliberately cultivate inefficiency. Time also comes to matter during processes of decomposition – the disintegration of modern narratives and logics can never be quickly mastered once and for all. Thus, in Narancay garden, as in most of the other gardens, there are many instances in which we intentionally slow down and cultivate attentiveness.

As we have mentioned in other chapters, slowing down is not easy. In Narancay, caring with soil as alive means working and attuning with a multitude of temporalities simultaneously. Perceiving soil temporality as homogeneous and static oversimplifies its complexity, reducing soil to a lifeless entity, whereas in reality, soil encompasses a multitude of timescales that are often interconnected and constantly evolving.

Attending to the temporalities of care and their slow labour can be a tiresome and mundane practice that demands dedication; it can be boring and thus not practiced, so it requires a shift in rhythm that can feel demanding, especially when one is used to outcomes-based schooling modelled after fast-paced capitalism.

As the children and Ximena slow down and begin reconfiguring their rhythms and collective movements, they discover an intricate system of tunnels. The tunnels are a site of mystery and wonderment: "Who made them?" "Why are they here?" "What stories do they tell?" Tunnels become the entry points for micro-cosmoses underneath the soil. We approach these tunnels as slow soil-making processes that enable a multiplicity of encounters across species. Insects share paths, interrupt flows, and connect as they move through the cylindrical space. We witness partial openings with this slowness as Ximena and the children encounter old eucalyptus roots emerging from the ground. The deliberate processes of tunnelling, as evidenced by the time it takes for roots to form, serve as a reminder that unlike the swift rhythms of large-scale agriculture on the surface, rooting is a patient and deliberate endeavour. This unhurried approach, gleaned from our reconnection with soil, resonates with Puig de la Bellacasa's (2015) exploration of care as an interrogative practice. Tunnelling prompts us to adapt our pace with a caring ethos and to wonder about how we might deeply care for soil.

In Narancay, we compose our pedagogical practices in attentive resistance to fast and normative temporalities that would ask us to move on quickly, to keep the transitional tempo that is set by developmentally appropriate practices. We resist this. To articulate this resistance, we need to work hard at carefully noticing what is emerging and what is addressing us. We need to imagine responsive pedagogical processes that are infused in composing pedagogical vitality. We invent, try out, and work with the generative creative force of improvisation. We try out pedagogically, affectively (rather than effectively), and aesthetically as we work hard to stay close and care for soil. In these doings, we introduce soil on sheets of parchment paper to see soil differently, to notice differently, and to create a sensorial intimacy with it, one that might open us to surprise (Puig de la Bellacasa, 2017). In doing this, we resist the urge to solidify understanding into rigid categories; instead, we invite an approach of resonating collective movement and imaginative micro-worlds alongside soil (Ingold, 2011). On the paper's smoothness, soil appears different: Its beautiful dark colours are highlighted; soil gains complexity as its small grains are made visible; it becomes more slippery; it gains movements and, with them, possibilities. Soil sticks to the children's hands, affording a visibility that would otherwise be taken for granted. Unexpectedly, tiny worms emerge moving at different speeds, some exposed and altered as they move out from the paper. We witness soil's liveliness and vulnerability and feel the implications of having gathered some soil on a different surface. These two points are consequential to what it means to care for the soil as alive.

The children create innumerable soil patterns and pathways that compose and decompose into indistinguishable lines serving as a reminder of soil's fluidity and movement and of the need to engage with it in alternative ways.

## Composting Pedagogies Require Care

As Haraway (2016) explains, in a compost community, restoration and care of ecological connections are central tasks. Likewise, composting pedagogies nurture themselves through practices of care. Again, Puig de la Bellacasa's (2019) writings, this time on soil care, are helpful for thinking composting pedagogies. Bellacasa insists that because "soils are living worlds" (p. 392), we have a response-ability to work together in caring ways – such care, she cautious, needs to extend beyond soil's "agricultural or industrial value" (p. 392). Soil care rather involves working *with* soil's livingness. Further, she proposes five affectively charged motifs of intimate entanglement with soil aliveness: biological wonder, interdependent livingness, sensual enlivenments, life as regeneration and animatedness" (p. 392). Composting pedagogies energize themselves by staying close to these forms of care relations. Further, they share with Bellacasa an ethical stance that the documentation embeds, to wit: "how to confront the commodification of soil life" (p. 393). Bellacasa's hope "is that looking at soils from the angle of affections entertained with them, of how soils intimately entangle humans into a new sense of material common aliveness, might nurture the ongoing search for more caring human-soil relations" (p. 393).

In the garden, paying attention to soil's minor changes becomes one of our ways to *affect*ively entangle ourselves with soil. For us, figuring out how to care for soil involves close encounters: *feeling it, tasting it, sensing it*. Caring for soil requires a slowness that is difficult to vitalize, as slowing down, focusing on particular details to imagine, takes patience. The children place their hands on the ground; they play with the soil, getting closer and closer. In this attending and aesthetic feeling, children's perceptions expand. After hours spent noticing the little cylindrical openings that are tunnelling down into the soil, a devil's coach-horse beetle nearby begins to dig, and the children realize they are meeting one of the makers of the tunnelling system. This encounter brings with it a disposition and openness towards many more encounters with other tunnel makers. The presence of the holes and the inaugural encounter with the devil's coach-horse beetle alludes to something unknowable in our experiences of soil. This unknowability proves to be transformative for everyone in the Narancay garden, as human-soil relations become charged with affective and ethical significance (Puig de la Bellacasa, 2019). In moving beyond mere scientific categorizations of soil – such as viewing it solely as a repository of harmful germs, bacteria, and viruses – we contemplate soil ethically as a practice of care that nurtures composting livingness.

## Composting Pedagogies Invite Speculative Gestures

We return here to Haraway's (2016) composting practices quoted above. To repeat, she says: "the richest humus for their inquiries turned out to be sf – science fiction and fantasy, speculative fabulation, speculative feminism, and string figures. Blocking the foreclosures of utopias, sf kept politics alive" (p. 150). In Narancay, speculative gestures of the kind that Haraway plays with abound. Speculative gestures, Haraway writes, involve "real stories that are also speculative fabulations and speculative realisms" (p. 10). These are stories, she continues, "in which multispecies players, who are enmeshed in partial and flawed translations across difference, redo ways of living and dying attuned to still possible finite flourishing, still possible recuperation" (p. 10). The speculative gestures that take place in the garden keep composting pedagogies politically engaged, nurturing the possibility of thinking otherwise.

We foster this political engagement by carefully noticing and working, in speculative ways, with the lively and ongoing movements that connect the under-above worlds in this garden. The tunnels that children encounter allude to a world that, as we mentioned, does not follow simplistic temporalities. Motivated by life in the soil, children encounter bacteria, fungi, and earthworms and engage with the many lives we can't see as we witness the decomposition process. Using pastels, watercolours, and soil as languages for tracing and finding pathways, we reconfigure relational logics by animating the creatures of the soil. A worm-like design transforms when painted. Red and blue legs are added to help the new insect move faster as it morphs into a centipede. In this combination of pencil drawings and water colour, stories emerge on how worms are in relationship with the insects that live above, below, and in-between the "underground border." As children draw and paint, they create stories that compose and decompose what is taking form. Animal patterns shift; threads of stories bring other threads. We are intrigued by all these co-compositions and how they keep deepening conditions to rethink human-soil relations in ways that liberate soil from its subjugation to human extractive logics and recognize it as a vibrant and sentient entity essential for the flourishing of all life. These speculative moments slowly bring generative doubt as the fluidity of the watercolour, soil's uncontained character, and the emerging ideas unsettle limits, borders, and dichotomies. For us, these pedagogical processes echo Haraway's (2016) words when she writes:

> We are provoked to think about pedagogical processes that might bring us closer to soil … Playing games of string figures is about giving and receiving patterns, dropping threads and failing but sometimes finding something that works, something consequential and maybe even beautiful, that wasn't there before, of relaying connections that matter, of telling stories in hand upon hand, digit upon digit, attachment site upon attachment site, to craft conditions for finite flourishing on terra, on earth. (Haraway, 2016, p. 10)

Ximena and the children imagine the multitude of lives and histories existing within the soil and notice how these stories can't be neatly encapsulated by narratives of productivity and progress or by discourses that view soil as valuable solely for its productivity. Spending significant time exploring tunnels and their "interdependent livingness" within the soil reveals the diverse array of lives thriving within it. Through drawing, watercolours, and pastels the children imagine what the insects and microscopical bacteria and protozoa actually do. How do they move? How might we need to move with the critters that make up soil? We resist an innocent stance on caring for the soil. This is a refusal to understand ourselves as caretakers with total agency and complete answers regarding simplified mechanical understandings of care with the soil.

In this proximity to soil, the children realize that tunnels are fractures in what initially appears to be a homogenous soil space. Tunnels lead us to wonder about different paths and how they move with lifeforms in the soil. Tunnels also lead to what is inaccessible, particularly when the soil – composed of a multitude of memories and temporalities – is so compact. Tunnels aerate the soil, but they also improvise with the soil as critters move around rocks and compact areas. In this way, tunnels and soil are interchangeable; singularly they are partial worlds working off of each other. We take up tunnels with what Puig de la Bellacasa (2019) describes as a "metamorphic re-arousal of a vital force" (p. 403), one that rejects mechanistic relations with soil and instead embraces a mysterious and animatory approach to sensual nature-culture entanglements.

Imaginative speculation of what is underneath the soil's surface gives us a possible entryway into imagining a different world to care for, one that decentres human agency and understanding (Puig de la Bellacasa, 2017). It invites us into a different way of being with soil, one that doesn't hold its production or output as a priority (Puig de la Bellacasa, 2017). Imaginative speculation is the pedagogical force in this garden, particularly on occasions where falling back into "schooling as usual" (with science and factual application about soil and decomposition) feels simpler and much more seductive or in moments where things seem stuck. In these moments, we attempt as much as possible to imagine what Puig de la Bellacasa describes as a "spirit of soil" and engage in speculative thinking as a "commitment to seek what other worlds can be made in caring" (Puig de la Bellacasa, 2015, p. 204).

To imagine a life with bacteria and protozoa, the children amplify their size with pastel images. As they hang the large drawings and notice how the wind moves them, microbes from below ground begin to have a narrative life above ground.

This form of vitality as the children work with tunnels and imaginary critters to speculate the below-ground world could be witnessed as anthropomorphic, but Puig de la Bellacasa (2019) argues that describing a speculative version of soil as an anthropomorphic projection is in fact giving humans too much credit. Bellacasa provokes us to keep the animation of soil as a relational question of "who animates whom" in more-than-human soil communities (p. 403). She argues that working with the soil's animatedness "open(s) [one] up to a sense of earthy connectedness that not merely animates and re-affects objectified worlds, but both intensifies and complicates a sense of ecological belonging for the humans involved" (p. 403). In Narancay, working speculatively in the middle between the above-ground and underground emphasizes this belonging and interrupts the notion of the human as a closed self. Speculation encourages composting pedagogies that create conditions to go beyond an egocentric and self-contained focus and reposition our humanity as humus in ongoing composting.

Composting pedagogies, then, engage in processes of composing and decomposing "as compost, finally [buries] under the ground, in the humus, the human body politic that has always elevated itself above the body of nature" (Timeto, 2021, p. 324). What then might have emerged from processes of decomposition and composition in Narancay? More provocatively, what might we have pedagogically composted with children and Ximena in the garden with the remnants of the magnificent Narancay gardens? As we read and reread the documentation, we are taken by how children immersed themselves in the soil, blurring the boundaries they had established when they found the holes in the ground. To be clear, we do not mean that composting pedagogies celebrate opportunities for children to experience sensory-rich explorations. In contrast to these developmentally appropriate dogmas, composting pedagogies are much riskier, more laborious, and less pretentious. What we mean instead is that in Narancay, the children, Ximena, and we re-emerged – always in unending and uneven ways – as composted subjects with unclear borders in unexpected relationalities and in kinship with soil.

# 7 The Aesthetics of Darkness, Light, and Distortion: Inventing and Reinventing in Challuabamba Garden

WITH ALEX BERRY

Figure 7.1. Speculative Drawing: Challuabamba Garden

Situated where Cuenca's city valley ends and the highland mountains begin, Challuabamba is a meeting place of temporalities and existences. Here, Cuenca's expanding contemporary suburbia meets longstanding Andean farmlands. The Pan-American highway moves through

Challuabamba, edging both ultramodern concrete housing developments and traditional adobe homes made of clay soil and grasses. Challuabamba is figured by the meetings of these coexisting Andean realities. In Challuabamba garden, teachers and the children encounter insects and creatures whose pathways gesture toward an underside of Challuabamba (https://viraltimes.climateactionchildhood.net/index.php/gardens/challuabamba_eng/). Speculating together about what exists below the garden, we meet an already living world. Like de la Cadena (2019), we hesitate to apply anthropocentric classifications of this place that might silence otherwise forms of life. Rather, we attempt to become sensitive to the "worlding capacity" of our collective excesses with creatures of the underworld who exceed our categories and classifications. Storying this world alive through poetic experimentations together with the children, we create pedagogical processes that open up new ways of being together in a place that is shaped by shadows and the unseen.

The emergence of Challuabamba's pedagogical processes is predicated on the dispositions of the educator, Goty, who thinks with, and intensifies, the distortions and divergences of the underworld as told through the children's stories. The pedagogical collaborations of pedagogista Cristina Delgado Vintimilla and atelierista Sylvia Kind (2021) inspire our attention to symbiotic mutuality as an orientation to curriculum; we consider curriculum as what they call an "ecology of participation" that is "embodied, relational, enactive, performative, and material" (p. 38). These curricular ecologies shape, and are shaped by, *fields of experience* or curricular situations that seek to generate new forms of togetherness with children and others (Vintimilla & Kind, 2021). The fields of experience we create in Challuabamba garden are specific to the life of this garden. The specificity of the Challuabamba garden is shaped by a co-presence of coloniality in the Andes, its modernist renovations, and ancestral sensitivities that continue to thrive in the garden. As de la Cadena (2015) reminds us, ongoing colonial presences in the Andes are maintained through anthropocentric logics of autonomy and separation. These logics are lived alongside time-honoured Andean knowledges that centre symbiosis and deep relationality above and below the land.

## Encountering Challuabamba's Underworld

Challuabamba garden is situated in a beautifully manicured landscape that surrounds a newly remodelled contemporary hacienda in the mountains skirting Cuenca. The original home was built using adobe, a traditional form of construction that combines clay soil and natural grasses and has been recently updated with a modern concrete exterior. Out in the yard with a small group of children, we are pulled into the children's proposition that "living things live underneath things." We see the children's interest in the underside of the garden as a possible figure that might help us to undo the "up side" of this beautiful yard behind the modern house and the human world that accompanies it. The children's proposition to consider an already living world underneath the modern garden opens us up to encounter the garden as a site of coexistence, a place that holds immense possibility for a curricular project that seeks to complexify prevailing imaginaries of the human as autopoetic or autonomously self-producing (Haraway, 2016).

Taking the children's proposition of an underneath world seriously, Goty creates an aesthetic invitation for herself and the children using a cover of thick dark fabrics, shadows, and small lit candles placed among bundles of drawing materials as a situation for initiating proximity to the garden's underworld, a place the children envision as shaped by darkness and many small fires.

In the distinct context of the pandemic's pause, the emerging pedagogical conditions initiated by our collaborations with Goty betray the rush of a typical day at school, with its subject divisions and recesses. Instead, children and educators spend long hours immersed in darkness, listening and intimately composing and living out this underworld. In this sense, the pandemic's interruption affords a certain temporality in the garden and a unique opening to refuse the neoliberal rhythms of modernity's temporal refrains (Stengers, 2008). In the context of the traditional educational structure, these refrains were lived through a daily flurry of brief, tightly scheduled, teacher-led activities and rapid transitions. Vintimilla and Pacini-Ketchabaw (2020) describe the sort of opening or radical interruption of the typical mode of schooling afforded by the pandemic as "the vital void of indiscernibility," where pedagogy can be thought with and experimented with (p. 635). As we have written elsewhere, we are interested in this void or peripheral space as a site of excess that might be generative for coming to sense new ways of being at the school (Berry et al., 2020).

## Sympoiesis: Making-With Children's Stories

As shown in the pedagogical documentation of Challuabamba garden (https://viraltimes.climateactionchildhood.net/index.php/gardens/challuabamba_eng/), the children's radically inventive stories of the underworld are at the heart of this inquiry. Their richly developed characters distort our perceptions of bodies through relational forms, logics, and codependencies. The children's stories are multilayered and co-composed with a series of shifting protagonists: the formless human without vision who relies on a centipede's guiding antennae; a spider who lends eyes to others to gather food; a scorpion who relies on the centipede's legs to run; a butterfly who loses its wings to the centipede. Listening to the children's stories we notice that in the underworld limbs are not static or sedimented on an individual body but rather they move across multiple bodies in differential and responsive ways. We attune to the distinct nature of each character as told through the children's stories using artistic mediums such as drawing, painting, and sculpting; the stories become material sites for imagining and performing new forms of togetherness. With de la Cadena (2019), by sustaining the singularities of each character, their divergence becomes a constitutive force of the pedagogical processes taking shape in the garden. The distinct qualities of each creature's limbs and their proposed ability to inventively outreach themselves to the unique needs of others is the basis of their collective survival. Yet, as Haraway (2016) reminds us, these lively symbiotic configurations are not synonymous with mutual benefit or neutrality (p. 60). The distinct systemic webbings of the children's underworld ecologies emerge as a consequence of uneven mutualities and co-contaminations, and they demand new modes of interpretation and expression. In creating Challuabamba garden's pedagogies, we attempt to take up this demand. In our pedagogical collaborations with Goty, we think with Whitehead's question, as read through Stengers (2008): "What are our modes of abstraction doing to us?" (p. 51). Through what speech or script might we communicate mutualities in the garden? With these questions at heart, together we try out new semiotic vocabularies that engage with the underworld's viral networks, beyond our all-too-human image (Latour, 1993).

In this spirit, the children's stories do not matter only because of their content. The pulse of the pedagogical work in Challuabamba garden is instigated by *how* the children's stories emerge and deepen alongside the educator's pedagogical interpretations and the pedagogical processes they make possible. It is this dependency between the stories themselves (the what) and their processes of formation (the how) that provokes our pedagogical collaborations (Vecchi, 2002). Becoming attentive to how the stories transpire, why they matter, and what pedagogical processes we can initiate to further materialize them (Vintimilla & Kind, 2021) is the basis of our work with Goty in the garden. This work requires a consistent revisioning of what is pedagogically significant to the educator (Rinaldi, 2021) and a careful attunement to the ways in which our interpretations, or modes of abstraction and expression

(Stengers, 2008), move in/out of modernity's territorial refrains – especially their allegiances with developmental psychology's autonomous, freely acting human.

Given careful attention, the making of these collective stories attempts to interrupt familiar educative rationalities that amend a neoliberal individuality. Rather, with particular curricular situations that are activated by Goty (Vintimilla & Kind, 2021), the stories of the underworld become sites of generative democratic exchange that take intimate multispecies dependencies seriously. These exchanges are preceded by Goty's emerging desire for dissensus, dialogue, and contamination as conditions for such a democracy. Thinking with how Walcott (2021) read Derrida, we envision the forms of democracy we engage with in Challuabamba garden, not as something we can attain or one day achieve, but rather as always to come and as a collective reorientation that is "both belated and always just ahead of us" (p. 5). Considering the temporal nature of our pedagogical collaborations as tentative and in the making (Pacini-Ketchabaw, Vintimilla, et al., 2020), we encounter Goty's educative desire as it ebbs and flows in response to the moving refrains of developmentalism's presence in the garden and the elasticity of its baseline within the school's shifting culture of education (Berry et al., 2020). Though the garden and its distance from the material and cultural conditions prior to the itinerant school afford a sense of liberty for experimentation within the pause of the pandemic, a prevailing desire for the advancing individual is reproposed through Goty's written notations and documentation of the children's experiences in the garden.

The initial documentation of the garden's underworld storied a sequential narrative of "what happened" in the children's inquiries and the developmental milestones they were reaching as a result of these activities. The underworld was quickly appropriated into a world for the developing child, viewed through existing frames that perpetuated colonial visions of the child as an explorer of this unknown place (Taylor, 2013) equipped with the innate creative ability to master it through certain skills and a practice of "collaboration" toward progress (Vintimilla & Berger, 2019). Significantly, the underworld was not yet imagined as a place where Goty herself was immersed, as her interpretations focused solely on observing and recording the children's actions. Together with Goty, we began considering how, as an educator, she could become a co-shaper of these stories. Co-creation requires a different role than only observing children's doings and providing them with experiences (Nxumalo et al., 2018). In an attempt to implicate Goty in the life of the underworld, we invited her to experiment with poetry as a way of writing herself into being with this new world. These poems initiated Goty's interpretive engagement with the underworld and the children's theories of this place in diffractive and experimental ways.

### *Sympoetics as Pedagogical Exploration*

In Challuabamba garden, the children's inventions provoke us to create pedagogical processes that engage with what Haraway might call the "oxymoronic" existence of underworld relations. When exercised through the concept of sympoiesis, collective poetry writing among Goty and us becomes a pedagogical exploration that activates a disposition of the educator required to engage with such a coexistence – an attuned responsivity to the productive difficulties proposed through a world we do not yet know and cannot contain. We view this poetry writing as pedagogical because it initiates a circumstance for educators to interpret educational events in speculative ways, opening up perceptions capable of engaging with the unforeseeable qualities of the underworld, its relational force, and its potential educational significance.

Poetry becomes a way of rewriting the prevailing categories of the human that withstand us (de la Cadena, 2019), enabling us to experiment with pedagogies that attempt to undo oppositional binaries that spatially and hierarchically divide and classify the world: above-under; inside-outside; dark-light; human-nonhuman; good-bad; self-other. Poetry writing stimulates both this disruption and, importantly, a tentative remaking of our subjective approximations to the underneath world as a site of curricular invention – one that is shaped through the divergences of multiple distinct and coexisting characters. Attempting to symbolically animate our mutual excesses with the underneath world through poetry, we experiment with pedagogical dispositions that engage with the productive irritations of "being with what we are not" (de la Cadena, 2019, p. 480, emphasis in original).

### *Making Poetry in Challuabamba Garden*

In writing poetry with Goty, we notice how language can be a device to make visible, discern, and rethink subjective processes (Braidotti, 2022). We mark up our poems with interruptions and provocations, and a diffractive dialogue emerges in the remaking of these poems. Writing, sharing, and collectively editing poems that seek to ideate the underneath world makes visible how our interpretations are already deeply contaminated by the categories of thought that structure a modern existence (de la Cadena, 2019). For instance, in reading our poems aloud, we notice how the underworld is consistently envisioned as a separate space from the world above, a place to individually master and eventually escape toward intrinsic truth and freedom. Below is an excerpt from one of Goty's poems that speaks to this desire for escape.

> We are all ignorant at birth, but we can explore the way out of the shadows, breaking paradigms that tie us to the shadows ... Our limitations are not economic, social, physical, they are cognitive. Our greatest enemy is within us and we only depend on ourselves to get out of that great shadow, that world below.

Through these readings, a narrative arises that speaks to the underneath world as a place that exists as an instructive lesson for humans to cognitively release themselves from "bad" shadows that "hold them from the light" – a world that is detached from the real and tangible life above. The darkness that figures this world is framed as something for the children to triumph over and become liberated from – in Goty's words, a movement "toward the light." Though the children are in deep conversation with the problems of a highly agentic underneath ecology, the educator's readings of these experiences remain tied to what the underneath world can do "in" and "for" the child. Read aloud, the poems make visible how colonial formations of the human continue to play out in the educator's desires of the underneath world, reaffirming Cartesian dualisms underwritten by the figure of the white, heterosexual, rational man as separate and superior. In these initial poems, the human can exist only despite, not because of or with, the underneath world.

With an attention to this dominant figure of the conquering human who uses mind over matter to master uncertainty (Tuck & Yang, 2012), we set out to stay with the tensions of the underneath world and its potential as a place of intense disturbance and mutation in order to unsettle the conceptual categories we use to imagine ourselves and our bodies. We think together about how our interpretations may perpetuate the binary logics we set out to disrupt and what the notion of sympoiesis might do to our poetic fabulations. We attempt to cultivate with Goty an emerging pedagogical desire to "learn with" the underneath world (Common Worlds Research Collective, 2020), a desire that unsettles escapism and engages with representational dissociations proposed through darkness (Blas, 2012). Our poems become instructive in returning us to the uncertainties of the garden's underworld with its complex mutualities and to take seriously the children's speculations so that we too might think and make "real" – strange – other ways of living.

### *Orientations to Poetry Writing and the Creation of Challuabamba's Pedagogies*

In Challuabamba garden, poetry brings a particular quality of writing that immerses us in the intimacies and struggles of interpretation and, however incompletely, the pedagogical desires these interpretations speak with. With Goty, poetry writing becomes a form of paying attention to what Walcott (2021) might call the subjective residuals of modernity's human. In the garden, this human is often unwittingly and insistently infused in educative desires and, consequently, pedagogical decisions. As we've discussed, poetry writing enables us to make perceptible how prevailing frameworks of the human show up in the garden's emerging pedagogies and how these logics may unwittingly figure our interpretations of the children's stories of this place. Yet, as a practice of creation, poetry is not only about deconstructing humanist discourses that hinder the irrational affective force of the underneath world; it also asks us to make something with what is brought into view. In our pedagogical explorations, poetry writing activates a push and pull between tongues – opening ways of perceiving and communicating that are less paralyzed by developmental discourse. Some key orientations shape poetry writing as a significant part of our pedagogical exploration and creation of Challuabamba garden's pedagogies.

First, poetry writing is not self-reflective. In our collaborative writings with Goty, we are intentionally wary of ideas of poetry as a self-making practice of the rational autonomous human. Rather, we view poetry making as part of a pedagogical process that is shaped with moving constellations of social, political, earthly, and technological forces at play in subjective formation. In this sense, poetry is not a form of writing that reflects the world as it was previously perceived. Rather, we attempt to think with poetry writing as a minor act of "making-with" (Haraway, 2016) and as the apparatus through which we come into the presence of the garden's underneath world ecology. With Deleuze, our poetic figurations do not involve grand claims or applications. Rather we attempt to centre what is preconceptual and "not yet" by writing to subtle and reciprocal junctures of thought and action (Colebrook, 2002).

When read through the lens of sympoiesis, we envision poetry writing as a way of narrating the multiple minor, *partial connections* (Haraway,

2016) that characterize underneath world pedagogies, where the notion of connectivity is not given or predetermined by the past but an emergent "matter of coming into existence" (Stengers, 2008). In very modest ways, poetry writing in Challuabamba garden asks us to make-with a temporality that is not reflective of a past but rather attempts to engage with what Cusicanqui (2018) describes as the spirals of Andean time, a temporality that is at once past, present, and future. Attending to the spiralling force of regression and progression that frames temporality in the Andes (Cusicanqui, 2018), poetry writing with Goty unsettles prevailing forms of pedagogical observation and narration in that it gives form to daily events with children beyond a literal or sequential mirroring of "what happened" – or a past simply brought forth to the present. With the real acknowledgment that our modes of abstraction have material consequences (Stengers, 2008), we attempt to thicken our semiotic codes beyond the reductive telling of a linear series of events so that we might carefully and ethically bring something "more-than" ourselves (Todd, 2001) into the pedagogical processes that figure our togetherness in Challuabamba garden.

Second, a poem, written or read, is an act of creation in its own right. In Challuabamba garden, writing and reading poetry is not an add-on or explanatory tool to sum up or represent our inquiries with children to others, nor is it an act of meaning making. Alternatively, we view our poetry as a practice of creation and research (Manning & Massumi, 2014) – where experience is recomposed via the language used to interpret and live it anew. As Leggo (2005) suggests, through poetry we write ourselves and the worlds we live into being. As an attempt at rendering the affective traces of an experience into symbolic form, poetry becomes an act of creation made in the making of a text, rather than merely an add-on description that is put on top of an experience already had (van Manen, 1990). As Griffin (1995) writes, "poetry does not describe. It is the thing. It is an experience, not the secondhand record of an experience, but the experience itself" (p. 191).

The practice of collectively writing, editing, re-editing, and reading aloud our poems activates a playfulness with vocabularies that gives sense to the most subtle, ephemeral qualities of our experiences with children in the underneath world that might otherwise fall beneath mention: *the sound of butterfly's broken wing, touch of spider's pedipalp, a sonic rush of the dark river*. For us, such poetic phrasings do not hold or even exercise meaning, but rather they produce multiple minor and indeterminate sensations. In this sense, reading a poem, much like encountering an art piece (Bishop, 2006, 2012), produces unique affectual resonances that do not precede but emerge upon encounter. The speculative quality of poetic writing calls on us to speak with what affects us and, with de la Cadena (2022), its excesses. To *feel* the limits of our experience and to make present what emerges beyond those limitations (p. 447). Thus, we write both to the actual and the virtual – something of the moment, tangible, felt, and lived – while also writing to the unintelligible propositions that the moment suggests and brings into existence. Poetry, then, can be understood as what Stengers (2005) calls an act of thinking-feeling-writing, and thus it has a fundamentally co-contaminative nature as the subject is always becoming "in the presence of" something else.

The orientations above enabled poetry writing to become a generative force for configuring an emerging pedagogical sensitivity to symbiosis, divergence, and speculation as constitutive qualities of Challuabamba garden's underneath-world pedagogies. Writing, editing, and (re)reading poetry collectively is a practice that holds us accountable to what becomes perceptible on paper and allows us to become "situated within the situation" that we are confronted with (Stengers, 2008, p. 51). In response to this perceptibility, we attempted to invent vocabularies, symbolic animations, even dramatizations (Stengers, 2008) through our poems that sought new bases and dissociations from the autonomous, rational human of development that haunts. Sustaining our obligation to create sympoietic textual modes, we engaged with poetry writing as an interpretive practice poised between human and more-than-human presences. Experimenting with words, their activations and translational limitations enabled new modes of approximation to the unique life of Challuabamba garden during the pandemic and, importantly, to its unintelligibility. Writing a phrase of poetry on paper expanded a capacity to sense the garden, a small gesture that rendered the garden at once more tangible and more elusive. We find this contradiction pedagogically significant because it relocates us into states of being that provoke our sensibilities beyond existing frames, "without protection" (Stengers, 2005). Within the distinct context of the itinerant school amid the pandemic's opening, poetry writing became an apparatus for paying attention differently to what matters in an educational experience – for attuning to what moves us and what moves beyond our words.

# 8 Weaving Proximity with Spiders: San Joaquín of the Weavers Garden

WITH ALICJA FRANKOWSI

Figure 8.1. Speculative Drawing: San Joaquín of the Weavers Garden

San Joaquín is a neighbourhood of contradictions. Affluent gated communities and high-end vacation rentals contrast with older areas where farmers, artisans, and weavers live and work in close relationship with the nearby Yanuncay river and its more-than-human inhabitants.

Inside the walls of a San Joaquín gated community is a garden that is part of the itinerant school, namely San Joaquín of the Weavers garden. As in the other gardens of the itinerant school, here the question of the human becomes pedagogically significant. Unlike what takes place in the other gardens, though, in San Joaquín of the Weavers, children wrestle over how to challenge the technocratic human as the sole maker of the world. It takes time and careful pedagogical processes to open up possibilities for reconfiguring human agency and eventually imbuing a certain kind of humility within children. In this chapter, we offer *stickiness* as a concept and a doing, alongside the pedagogical documentation that narrates how children weave in proximity with spiders (https://viraltimes.climateactionchildhood.net/index.php/gardens/san-joaquin-2-eng/).

## Reorienting Pedagogical Processes: Expanding Notions of Pristine Nature

Attempting to echo San Joaquín's geo-political-social contrasts and contradictions, with Carolina, the teacher, we begin by emphasizing the garden's complex and less-than-pristine spaces. For us, attending to this complexity is a way to unsettle modern notions of nature as intrinsically beautiful and harmonious (as it is understood in many stewardship models of education; see Taylor, 2013). To this end, Carolina introduces the children to that which is often overlooked around the river. The children are quickly drawn towards the difficult relations Carolina points them towards. While spending time on the riverbank amid decaying eucalyptus stumps, for example, the children notice that life is abundant in what seems decayed. As Francisco remarks, "Those trunks are old eucalyptus trees, and although they are dead, they are full of life." The children are similarly intrigued by spiders' peculiar ways of living in the garden. They notice interesting disparities between them and spiders. For instance, while darkness is unsettling for them, spiders love the dark; in the absence of light spiders hide, hunt, and feed.

In this process of thinking in proximity with spiders, however, tensions emerge. Reading the documentation, we notice that children are quickly resorting to predefined technofixes or finding refuge in commonly accepted notions of human-animal interaction to "solve" the "problems" they encounter in contradiction. Deep frustration at a failed attempt to move swiftly like spiders across decayed tree stumps is the first indication that children might be stuck, not only in modern notions of human supremacy, but also in "a worldwide system of automatic connections in which individuals cannot experience conjunction but only functional connection" (Berardi, 2017, p. 116). Another hint is when children accidentally break a spider's nest and immediately respond by wanting to fix it or when they want to save spiders and other creatures from what they perceive as a challenging landscape. Further, they respond with distress when they attempt to act and feel like insects stuck in a web, and another time, they experience disillusionment when they cannot save an orphaned spider for which they carefully wove a new web. Their desire for happy endings as a response to the ambiguities of coexistence and mutual dependence – such as when they witness a beetle and a bee dying after being ensnared in a spider web – makes it glaringly obvious to us that we might need to reorient our pedagogical processes, not only towards problematizing human sovereignty – the human desire to fix problems or to act for the collective good – but also towards opening up the horizon of possibility (Berardi, 2017) in response to the impotence the children are experiencing.

To clarify, our intention is not to psychologize children by finding deficiencies in their thinking and proposing activities that will help them learn new ways of thinking. By learning new ways of thinking we mean creating opportunities for children's minds to undergo a transformative process, forming neural connections and acquiring knowledge that shapes their cognitive abilities, problem-solving skills, and eventually their emotional development. Such an approach is a significant departure from how we think and do education. For us, working pedagogically involves attending to processes of subject formation that, yes, are transformative but not theological nor deterministic. To explain, we proceed by considering Berardi's (2017) proposition that

> the present reality contains the future as a wide range of possibilities, and the selection of one possibility among many is not prescribed in a deterministic way… The future is inscribed in the present as a tendency that we can imagine: a sort of premonition, a vibrational movement of particles that are taken in an uncertain process of continuous recombination. (p. 13)

Returning to the inquiry rather than dismissing the struggles we encounter in children's responses, we decide to activate pedagogical processes to respond to these emerging challenges. In fact, it is in navigating these tensions that the pedagogical work in this garden takes place. In these difficult moments, and in our pedagogical dialogues about them, we begin to notice the limitations inherent in the emerging inquiry. An important question emerges in the midst of the inquiry: What pedagogical possibilities might we glean from the children's insistence on solving problems through technofixes? Engaging with this query, with Carolina we craft curricular trajectories, including a series of aesthetical explorations, that focus on the communicational impossibilities and incommensurabilities between children and spiders, spiders and insects, and children and webs. These explorations offer us the opportunity to engage in processes that intensify children's attention to collective tensions. Through these curricular trajectories, we draw inspiration both from spiders' delicate, sticky webbing and from the intricate techniques of San Joaquín's weavers. In this regard, we join "histories of thinking-making-writing-with spiders" (Price & van Eeden-Wharton, 2023, p. 180). Moreover, thinking with Price and van Eeden-Wharton (2023), a spider's web as a central figure "serves as an unsettled mapping-in-process and assemblage-in-action, supportive mesh, carrier bag, and sticky knot from which we reach forward and back" (p. 180).

## Sticky Moments in Proximity with Spiders

Having cast spiders and San Joaquín weavers as central figures in our pedagogical work, we then think with the metaphor of "sticky moments" to describe unfamiliar situations and inaccessible modes of understanding and communication. Inspired by the work of feminist scholars, stickiness, for us, "is avowedly relational – it binds us together in encounter, clings to us, travels with us. It is ambiguous, unpredictable, and uncomfortably in-between. Viscous and malleable, stickiness contrasts with rigidity, solidity, and stability" (Price & van Eeden-Wharton, 2023, pp. 189–90). The sticky moments we emphasize become impasses that defy easy resolution by the children. We invite the children to actively "weave" through these sticky moments, collectively embracing intuitive, responsive, and emergent processes rather than relying solely on technocratic solutions (Manning, 2016). That is, with stickiness we come to understand frustrating problems that we cannot quite let go of. Stickiness provides a pivotal way of understanding the difficulty of our work when we notice that children's responses are stuck in human supremacy – in putting human interests over others'.

Stickiness challenges our sovereign wanting and doings. The pedagogical processes in San Joaquín of the Weavers garden occasion encounters where children experience the limitations of their own grandiosity and, at the same time, open paths that reconfigure their field of action, pointing the children to a more humble approach to what they are capable of (Haraway, 2008). Haraway (2016) argues that the "inhabitants of the world, creatures of all kinds, human and non-human, are wayfarers" (p. 32). Her ideas help us to find resonances among spiders, children's movements, and the slow processes of weaving. We persist in thinking of weaving and the actions it creates as we encounter conflicts together and share failures to save spiders and other creatures. In this way, sticky moments, as we refer to them, become a commitment to collective work when we encounter difficulty, collision, or existential knots that need tenderness and care.

Stickiness is not without its difficulties: It often encounters resistance, creates moments of stagnation, discourages the children, leads them to express boredom (they are "bored of spiders," they say), sparks great doubts for Carolina and us, and so on. No doubt stickiness reminds us of the accompanying difficulties of slowing down, paying attention, and finding interest in proximities. What propositions invite us to stay and attend to what is difficult or boring? How, in these moments, do we negotiate our roles as teachers in relation to children's habits but also their desires? What processes might we invent and propose, to be able to persist, to stay, to come back again and again and learn with the spiders' lifeworlds? Sustaining attention to stickiness requires that we dwell in its resistance by fluctuating focus and/or leveraging setbacks.

## Weakening Human Mastery and Sovereignty

To work through stickiness also requires thoughtful conceptual work on our end. Opening up possibilities to think beyond human agency demands a shift away from neoliberal education models that emphasize individual agency by empowering children to make autonomous choices and that promote the notion of personal responsibility to address many of our current social and ecological challenges. To rethink agency as solely the domain of humans, we are inspired by anthropologist Ingold's (2022b) writings on meshworks. In his essay where a spider is personified, worth quoting here at length, Ingold not only shows that action extends beyond human capacity but also puts in question, for us, the scope of human influence or control in the world. Spider explains:

> The lines of my web … are themselves spun from materials exuded from my own body, and are laid down as I move about. You could even say that they are an extension of my very being as it trails into the environment – they comprise, if you will, my "wideware". They are the lines along which I live, and conduct my perception and action in the world. For example, I know when a fly has landed in the web because I can feel the vibrations in the lines through my spindly legs, and it is along these same lines that

> I run to retrieve it. But the lines of my web do not connect me to the fly. Rather, they are already threaded before the fly arrives, and set up through their material presence the conditions of entrapment under which such a connection can potentially be established. (Ingold, 2022b, pp. 91–2)

Spider's point is that "the web is not an entity."

> That is to say, it is not a closed in, self-contained object that is set over against other objects with which it may then be juxtaposed or conjoined. It is rather a bundle or tissue of strands, tightly drawn together here but trailing loose ends there, which tangle with other strands from other bundles. For the twigs or stems to which I attach these trailing ends are themselves but the visible tips of complex underground root systems. Every plant, too, is a living tissue of lines. And so, indeed, am I. It is as though my body were formed through knotting together threads of life that run out through my many legs into the web and thence to the wider environment. The world, for me, is not an assemblage of bits and pieces but a tangle of threads and pathways. Let us call it a meshwork ... My claim, then, is that action ... emerges from the interplay of forces that are conducted along the lines of the meshwork. (Ingold, 2022b, pp. 91–2)

The spiders' meshwork becomes a catalyst for our work with children that allows us to crack traditional notions of individual autonomy. To clarify, our approach is not to teach children that agency, as an interconnected phenomenon of both human and nonhuman entities, is fluid and encompasses the complex web of relationships and interactions within which agency emerges. Rather, we create conditions where we can experience and propose processes that trouble agency based on human individualism. We embrace the beautiful struggle to create processes that, as Ingold (2017) writes, "put the 'I' who acts not in front but in the midst of the experience undergone. And being in the midst, it is continually rediscovering itself" (p. 17).

## Weaving as a Practice of Proximity with the Spider

As we mentioned above, it is through weaving that we expose the children to the tensions and the stickiness that propel them beyond both human sovereignty and ideas of loss or inadequacy. The children carefully think with the spiders' techniques; they attempt to mimic the spiders' movements: falling over and tangling when attempting to cross the threads, creating circular structures similar to that of woven baskets instead of the intricate, symmetrical design of a spider web. At times frustrated, the children begin to admire the spider's precision and architectural prowess; using various mediums and techniques they try hard to gesture towards the delicate geometry of the web. It is at this time, "'in the midst of things' – situated and attached, but neither static nor settled; responsive and always involved" (Price & van Eeden-Wharton, 2023, p. 190) – that something different emerges. Tangled in yarn and trying to keep its tension, children realize that they are unable to weave a web like a spider; it is impossible, they say, because humans simply don't have spider silk in our bodies. Thus, it is "both in encounter and in (re)turning to encounters as [they] inhabit these experiences" (p. 194) that children come to inhabit the meshwork. These processes give form to pedagogies of humility and doubt – doubt in the face of human autonomous sovereignty and doubt also in discourses of mastery that characterize to such a great degree education and teaching. These pedagogies of doubt are difficult. They make us move away from, or be suspicious of, the confident assertions that try to keep human supremacy intact.

In the midst of this intricate work, Carolina leaves the school and Anita (who was already part of the garden) takes over the pedagogical work at San Joaquín of the Weavers. Weaving continues to intrigue and, at times, frustrate the children. Considering the importance of weaving for Cuenca, with Anita we put spiders' weaving into conversation with the work of women weavers in San Joaquín. The children are not completely unfamiliar with weaving; it is a practice they have been exposed to throughout Cuenca. In fact, they share many stories – initially about their families' weaving traditions and techniques and later about how we might translate them into spiderweb-weaving practices. These connections provide children an opportunity not only to inherit longstanding traditions that are at risk of eroding due to the area's rapid urbanization but also to engage with weaving as world making (that is, for the spiders, weaving as meshwork).

To explain, as the documentation narrates, the children virtually meet Ms. Rosario, a local weaver who makes baskets using *duda* (a local plant fibre). This is an important moment for the children as they experience Andean weavers' relationship with what they weave. Andean weavers are never separated from what they weave. As Arnold explains, "material things such as textiles, pots, or stones are not only part of these communities of living things, but living beings in themselves. Textiles are living beings ... the action of weaving converting material substance into a 'person'" (p. 143). In other words, weavers' subjectivity is in their textiles – material and immaterial substances are difficult to distinguish. This encounter with Ms. Rosario incites us to work with techniques of weaving as a practice for world making (rather than to make a product).

The children do not hesitate to embrace duda and Ms. Rosario's techniques. As children's fingers come to know the duda's singular quality (rounded rather than angular edges), they find new ways to weave a web, prompting new speculative stories that continue their fascinating conversations about the stickiness of the web. Some children, for example, imagine many spiders collaborating to create a square web, while others think of spiders using the morning dew left on leaves to soften the fibres of their webs.

These emerging experimental doings and undoings, makings and unmakings, thinkings in-between-with, and patternings and randomness, always inspired by the traditions of the place and its inhabitants, offer children the possibility to encounter spiders as unique weavers within intricate worlds, as well as to reencounter their own vulnerabilities. Thus, we might say, with Price and van Eeden-Wharton (2023), that San Joaquín of the Weavers became a pedagogical space "to dwell in sticky spaces, open to trouble; [and] to embrace unexpected knots and loose threads" (p. 196).

The destabilizing force that came with a shift – from regimes of certitude typical of traditional schooling towards trajectories of invention – pushed Carolina, Anita, and us into uncharted territory as we embraced the challenge of creating conditions for emergence. Carolina's intention to search for what was not readily visible, or what held tension and difficulty, was challenging under the current capitalist tendencies towards quick automation. It took careful pedagogical work for children to question their own agency within the garden's life and in relation to the more-than-human. Creating curricular trajectories that brought difficulties (such as attending to spiderwebs' stickiness and duda's demands) into sight and into mind in situ created possibilities for alternative world relations to emerge amid children's storytelling.

Importantly, children's noticing that human supremacy could damage and/or destroy more-than-human life was not imposed in the form of a lesson, nor was it morally communicated. It was pedagogically crafted through processes that attended to the tensions and conflicts that arose in children's relations with the world. Todd (2015) describes these types of response to conflicts or incommensurabilities as *traumatism* – a sensory disruption in our attempts to escape suffering that shifts our very holds on identity. This disruption, both in a traditional schooling model and in the ways the children and Carolina worked with each other, challenged humancentric roles often prioritized in schooling. Weaving, the garden, and storying different worlds in our weaving drew our imaginations closer to the spiders' movements in the garden while reminding us of our own limitations in entering the spiders' world. For us, this very realization invited a practice of humility on the part of the children.

# 9 Fluid Simulations in San Joaquín of the Yanuncay Garden

WITH ALICJA FRANKOWSKI

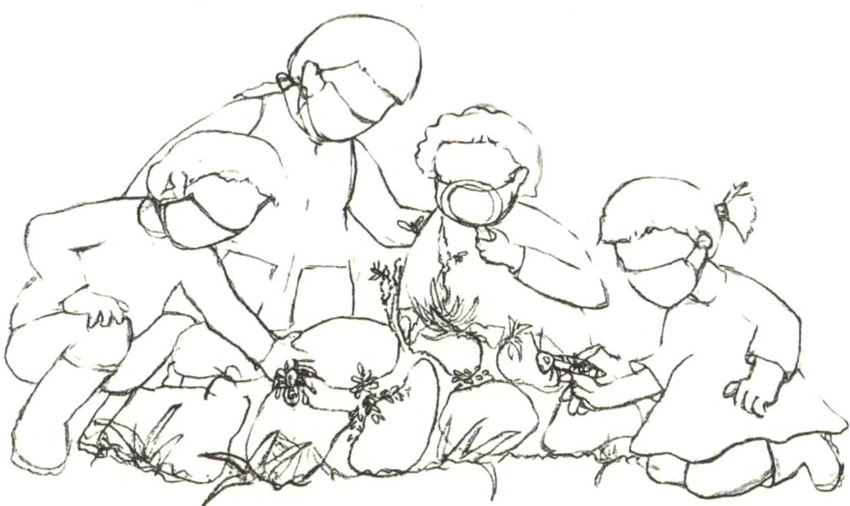

Figure 9.1. Speculative Drawing: San Joaquín of the Yanuncay Garden

Cuenca is a city of rivers – four rivers act as hydro-social connectors and as such become places of life and cosmic possibility (Deutsch Lynch, 2019, p. 45). One of these connectors, Yanuncay river, is in close proximity to the itinerant school's San Joaquín of the Yanuncay garden, and it became a pedagogical protagonist in the garden. With its headwaters in the Cajas mountains, Yanuncay travels forty-three kilometres, reaching the garden in its full potential. As the garden's pedagogical documentation shows, the teacher, Cris, welcomes the rich pedagogical possibilities that proximity to Yanuncay offers to the garden (https://viraltimes.climateactionchildhood.net/index.php/gardens/san-joaquin-1-eng/).

This is not a traditional schooling project, as what one might see, for instance, in a science class, where rivers are often depicted as isolated and independent elements. Cris challenges the ways in which modern and neoliberal education systems remove rivers' relationalities and, consequently, she disrupts the very Western nature/culture divide that such a treatment embraces (Taylor & Ketchabaw, 2017). In San Joaquín of the Yanuncay garden, Cris and the children think intimately *with* Yanuncay: to notice its relations, attend to its movements, experiment and play with them, and become part of the river's relationalities. This chapter narrates these stories in which, as the documentation shows, simulation and storytelling vibrate throughout.

## River Metaphors and Relations

Children join the river by physically bringing their bodies into relation with it. They experiment with how to find themselves in proximity with Yanuncay as they figure the possibilities this proximity might make possible. Cris and we are interested in pedagogical processes that might bring the children closer to the river and in ways that might foster their awareness of its alterity. The children witness and pay attention to the intermingling dance of stone, water, and light in the river, as well as how this relational dance animates the life of the river. To create processes that escape education's lack of attention towards the more-than-human's alterity requires undoing many dichotomies (e.g., nature-culture; human-animal; child-adult) as well as the deep fragmentation with which we treat disciplines and knowledges. Through these experimentations, children's bodies move away from the semantic fragmentary metaphors present in individual entities such as *piedra* (stone), *agua* (water), *luz* (light), *río* (river), and *niñe* (child). Instead, the river's vibrant movements imperfectly become a site for relations, not just among the "qualities of the river" (e.g., in the way these elements partially reflect the nearby trees) but relations that create rock-water-light-river-child compositions that articulate possibilities beyond each element's qualities. These compositions arise from acknowledging kinship and relationships forged in the children's playful fluidity of connections, mirroring the meandering flow of a river. As days pass in this garden, the river changes, and with that, children also shift as relations with themselves and others are dynamically reconfigured. Weeks go by and the boundaries the children encountered during the first visits to the river become much more difficult to find or sustain.

To be precise, as the children see themselves mirrored in the river, they notice Yanuncay's imprint on their hands. Light reflects off the water onto children's bodies, and the river's movements and reflections move with the children. In this way, Yanuncay is not only relational and situated but also embodied as its shape emerges through the children's bodies. These encounters alter conversations among the children, who, instead of addressing the river as a separate entity, "become the river." We read these playful movements as a metaphor and as corporeal experiences (MacLeod & Neimanis, 2013). Keeping in mind Lakoff and Johnson's (2003) conceptualization of metaphor as inseparable from experience, MacLeod and Neimanis (2013) write, "we cannot avoid thinking in metaphor, and that our thoughts are always structured by our bodily experiences" (p. 10). As children focus on the relational and transient properties of water, their emphasis on corporeal experience contradicts separative tendencies in schooling that isolate the sun or water from human beings. As we mentioned above, in Yanuncay garden, water-light-human-body transient formations disrupt Western fragmented notions of nature and culture. On one hand, water-light becomes engulfed in animism and is capable of acting on and "swirling" with the children as they sense the magical ways in which the elements work together in relation. On the other hand, a river full of life runs down the mountains, melds with light, and integrates into children's bodies.

## Compositions with the River

In collaboration with Cris, we amplify these animisms. We work with photography and video to intensify light waves diffracting and moving through human and more-than-human bodies. We focus on composing images and videos that show how the camera picks up rays of light as they touch the water, creating contradictions that spark movement and flow within each other, often leaving blank spaces and diamond-like figures. Working with these photographs and videos in the garden escalates our attention to the river's magic and, pedagogically, helps us to create an educational space that removes pedagogy from its traditional anthropocentric orientation. Thus, another pedagogical attentiveness is made possible here. This is an attentiveness not framed within human development and/or the achievement of sovereign human autonomy within a world made to be dominated. Instead, it is an attentiveness that brings to life the potential to renovate the educational coordinates of late capitalism and open pedagogical paths towards unusual and urgently needed alternative encounters in education.

Our engagements with the river in the garden open opportunities for encounters between the children and local artisans who continue the centuries-long practice of carefully crafting and recrafting pathways in the river through stone irrigation systems. These hydraulic systems, which ensure sufficient irrigation throughout the whole region, moderate the heavy rainfall characteristic of the Andes (Erikson, 2019, p. 37). As the children engage with the engineering of water systems, they are intrigued with how stones, water, and human interdependencies create Yanuncay. Stones, they chatter, are not a backdrop to the river: They are actively involved in the movements and currents of the water, the light reflections, and the liveliness of many nearby creatures. Once invisible to the children, the stones are now provocateurs of intense debate, especially around the deep relation between insects and the tiny cracks in the stones.

## Simulation in Curriculum Making

At times, Yanuncay is a trickster. As it carries water down from the mountains, it can swell and become inaccessible in an instant, without warning. Heavy rainfalls turn the river into a force unsafe to enter. During these times of shifting weather patterns and intensities, proximity to the river becomes limited, sometimes for weeks. Such big water flow events take place during the year of the itinerant school. Cris's pedagogical intention to become intimate with Yanuncay is reduced to mere droplets of nostalgic river memory. In conversation with Cris, in response to her frustration, we collectively bring Yanuncay and its relations to the garden. As we wonder how we might pivot our curricular processes and our pedagogical intention to be in close proximity to Yanuncay, we challenge our own assumptions about proximity. Proximity extends beyond physical presence. Then, we ask: How might the garden become a space for river encounters that do not rely on representational determinacy and that allow clarity and precision in the encounters? What kinds of sensations might emerge from thinking proximity beyond closeness in space? Can there be proximity in the dynamic between the virtual and the actual?

To engage with these queries, we contemplate the possibilities of simulation as a curricular focal point. Although our interpretation of the term *simulation* is closely associated with the work of French philosopher Baudrillard (1995), we use it somewhat loosely in our curricular work. Baudrillard refers to simulation as attempted imitations of reality and cautions about an easy fall into simulacra. For him, unlike simulation, simulacra refers to copies or representations of things that either have no original meaning and connection to reality or have lost them. For us, to engage in simulation of the river is to continue to imbue the river with meaning within children's lifeworlds. Keeping in mind Baudrillard's caution of a simulacrum condition, we work with relations to real lifeworlds aware that the river itself could suffer from a loss of meaning. That is, we are cautious that engaging in simulacra might easily remove children from Yanuncay and its relations rather than bringing them closer to it. In the garden, Cris welcomes what we refer to as a careful simulation of the river, that is, a simulation that resists representative narratives of Yanuncay. We stay with the tension that emerges as children attempt to fully represent the river or create a replica that is disconnected from Yanuncay.

Our decision to engage with simulation is driven by the children's willingness to think relationally, to step away from fixed conceptual determinisms and to be suspicious that everything starts in the "I." Pedagogically, we do not shy away from this willingness. We keep it close to our work because such willingness bursts with educational relevance. For us, the pandemic is an experience that demands we insist on creating a less egocentric educational experience, one that makes us much more aware of our profound entanglements within a life with others and within a world that cannot be reduced to the individualistic I. This educational experience is relevant for us because we, like many other scholars, do not reduce education to matters of teaching and learning. Importantly, this relevance also presents itself in light of the neoliberal times in which we live.

## Simulation Encounters

In the sheltered space of the garden, Cris and the children experiment with relational simulations of light, water, stone, and shadows. Children engage with water and light movements and tell stories about the inhabitants of this simulated river world. The allure of the sun and its influence on the water and the rocks repositions the children's own bodies' relations to water. Bodies crouch and micro-gestures respond to the constantly changing light formations. Slippery rocks press on feet, and balancing becomes a relational necessity to focus on a light that seems to slip from the children's hands. Acting together with the light, the children-water relations become an ever-changing dance of unpredictability. Over time, as the children continue to experiment with simulations, they engage in processes that blur the lines between magic and reality, natural and unnatural, animate and inanimate.

As we have mentioned, there is danger in playing with simulations. Aware of the risks of working pedagogically through simulations, we intentionally stay in close connection with Andean cosmologies, bringing their cultural relevance into the simulated river. In Andean cosmologies, according to Gose (2019), sun-water relations are circular as "the sun's fiery heat is not simply opposed to water ... but also sustained and increased by it as an animated substance" (p. 117). Gose writes, "By virtue of its heat the sun is able to accumulate and command water, driving its circulation within this cosmos as animating figures more powerful than other water-dependent beings" (p. 117). In our case, there is an appeal to moving with the light as the children attempt to manipulate it. In this way the sun, with its relations with the water and its work around the stones, is an animator abundant in energy exchange.

Resisting Cartesian material stability and shifting instead towards dynamism (Arnold, 2019, p. 143), we follow the partial light-stone-water relations to activate their transformative potential (Ingold, 2011). Akin to when we visit Yanuncay, in the garden the children bring lights to create unidentifiable shapes, and they notice how light and water act in unexpected ways on their bodies. In some instances, the children describe light structures as "monstrous" or "magical," while at other times – especially when encountering their shadows in the light – the light seems more proximal, and the children declare, "It is us!" As with Andean animations of cosmos, where the "world is composed of a succession of animating regimes" that are partial and temporally influenced (Gose, 2019, p. 118), these river-light animations shapeshift from one form to another. These minor relational movements reanimate the river and its relations, and the children's prior engagements with the river.

## Storytelling in Simulations

Pivotal in our work with simulations are storytelling practices and the imaginative figures that emerge through them. As Haraway (1991) suggests, storytelling as a practice imagines other possibilities for knowing. Storytelling helps us steer away from a universal understanding of rivers. Through storytelling, in contrast, children engage in complex and deeply relational stories with Yanuncay. Critiquing stories that privilege universal models, Haraway suggests that situated stories – she sometimes calls them cyborg stories – address the hybridity of relations. Cyborg storytelling, Haraway argues, challenges boundaries between nature and culture, human and nonhuman. The story fragments children tell allow a complex Yanuncay to emerge.

Through storytelling, the children also become cultural mediators of a constantly shifting Yanuncay they cannot visit. Children's daily experimentations with river simulations are stories of what might have happened if they were at the river. Storytelling becomes a space for remembering past encounters at the riverbanks mixed with creation work. In this mediation, bodies and the metaphors derived from engagements with monsters, shadows, light, darkness, magic, heat, and rain are protagonists. Particularly, we work with the tensions that emerge by amplifying the fluidity of light and its "leakiness" as children play with projections of light onto the wall, onto paper, onto water, and onto plastic. The fluid character of the light used as a medium not only helps to hold these contradictions at bay but also stories Yanuncay's fragmentary and fluid nature. That is, on one hand, this collective storytelling makes space for possible narratives. On the other hand, it keeps open the possibility that attempts at pure, objective representations of the river are unfulfilled. This tension makes the work of storytelling pedagogically significant. The stories that are singular to the pedagogical processes in this garden disrupt static representations of the river. In education such representations often strive for objectivity and accuracy. This is an idea that often comes up in our conversations with teachers in the itinerant school as we decide to allow ourselves and the children to make curricular trajectories based on the affective and multilayered nuance, ambiguity, and interpretative force that stories offer. This departure from fixed representations allows us to have conversations that challenge conventional notions of truth and authenticity, real and unreal, opening space for alternative narratives to be heard and valued.

As children reconfigure the world they simulate, they also reconfigure their own subjective realities. Through storytelling, they see their own "monstrosities" in the light and how they might be fundamental in the creation of alternative relations: "Now we are the monsters of the story" and "I can create the light and move the light," they utter as they reinsert themselves into the Yanuncay's water-light relations they attempt to simulate. There is always some sort of re-creation and re-animation in the storytelling that offer an imaginative supplement without moving into simulacra. Drawing, sculpting, and light-play offer these spaces for re-creation and re-animation. Moreover, children's moves towards augmenting, overlapping, distorting, morphing, reconsidering, and redrawing water-light-shadow-bodies relations suggest the impossibility of complete representation or, to quote Manning (2008), they suggest "the more than of its actual representation" (p. 328).

We might also suggest, drawing on curriculum theory, that the monstrous and ghostly enactments emerging in Yanuncay garden resonate with processes of *currere*. In currere, McNulty (2019) suggests, emergent memory work moves beyond the real into imagined desire. For us, this perspective highlights the transformative power of memory, which extends beyond mere recollection of past events. Monsters and ghosts, drawn to the shadows and deviations, serve to redefine human subjectivities, particularly in children's interactions with Yanuncay. By bridging the past with the future, the monsters and ghosts in children's tales awaken Cris to a life force that disrupts linear temporalities where memory projects into otherwise and unknown possibilities and, in that, it already makes a present that welcomes difference.

As Yanuncay's waters subsided, Cris and the children returned to it. This time, monsters appeared. The children noticed the trees bringing shade to the flowing rapids while they played to recreate the shadowy figures with their hands. The river transformed into a monstrous realm where light and shadow interplayed, shifting and morphing in tandem with the dynamic relationships among children's bodies, water, and light as they drew closer or moved apart.

The indomitable characteristics of light inspire us to think and enact relations that are always fluid and uncontained. Such relations are unpredictable and not easy to master. Yet, they are hospitable, far-reaching, and open to unexpected configurations.

# 10 Blanketing and Textures in River Encounters: Puertas del Sol Garden

Figure 10.1 Speculative Drawing: Puertas del Sol Garden

Hydrological relations abound in Cuenca. People's movements in the city are organized around the four rivers that crisscross the city, blanketing it with beauty and anxiety in equal measure. The Tomebamba, originating in the Cajas mountains, merging into the Amazon and ending up in the Atlantic Ocean, is one of the bodies of water that both sustain and constrain human and more-than-human life in Cuenca. What is certain is that this river is alive. Rushing waters containing energy from the high Andes trespass the carefully manicured parks during rainy seasons, while dry spells reveal the remnants of lives destroyed by strong currents now entangled within the Tomebamba's beautiful grey rocky surface. Spiritually and politically, the Tomebamba continues to nurture generations of local Indigenous and Mestizx peoples who have been taking care of this "wilful" river for millennia. As we write this chapter, the Tomebamba, like Cuenca's other rivers, is threatened by international mining corporation projects that promise financial gains to a struggling country. In fact, like other bodies of water, "today more than ever, rivers also are a major part of the toxic ecology of industrialization, modernity, and globalized consumer culture, carrying plastic and other pollutants such as waste pharmaceuticals to the oceans" (River Severn Estuary UK et al., 2021, p. 456). The possibility of a toxic Tomebamba divides Cuenca in the same way the river does.

This is the conflicted space embraced by the children in Puertas del Sol Garden (https://viraltimes.climateactionchildhood.net/index.php/es/jardines/puertas-del-sol-esp/) during the pandemic. Neither taking for granted the Tomebamba's presence nor avoiding its politically charged waters, Cecilia, the teacher, proposes pedagogical processes that reanimate and recreate children's relations with the Tomebamba. Creating opportunities for proximity, Cecilia carefully makes curriculum by bringing the river in all its complexity into visibility. At every turn, the Tomebamba's singularities resonate among the children. The Tomebamba is not akin to any river; its unique and shifting colours, sounds, stories, smells, speeds, rhythms, waste, inhabitants, and mood matter in the garden. We might say that relational pedagogies are carefully stitched in Puertas del Sol as one of the rivers that nurtures the city becomes a focal point for viral pedagogies.

This chapter narrates the pedagogical processes in Puertas del Sol Garden. They move alongside the pedagogical documentation curated in the Itinerant School website (https://viraltimes.climateactionchildhood.net/index.php/es/jardines/puertas-del-sol-esp/). The narratives focus on pedagogies that bring children into proximity with the Tomebamba river. While geographically the Tomebamba is a central presence in Cuenca, a close relationship with it is often taken for granted in educational contexts. We wonder what kind of pedagogical and aesthetic encounters might bring us closer to the river. What gestures of reaching out might we engage with? The river is there, always there, with its sound, and even when there is no water – no sound – the river is there. The river is a presence that is hard to ignore, yet we notice a relational absence among children, teachers, and the river. We choose not to read this relational absence as failure but as a lingering, insisting, and unavoidable possibility to be taken up in our work and micro-experimentations in this garden. To do so, children encounter the Tomebamba's singularity, as well as the histories, complexities, contradictions, and relations – both toxic and nontoxic – that make this river. Through multiple media (textiles, charcoal, watercolours), children connect with the Tomebamba's sound, fluidity, languages, memories, companions, and relations. By attending to the river's singularity, children not only become close to the river but also speculate on what they share with the Tomebamba.

## Encountering the Tomebamba River

Early in the curriculum-making process, in collaboration with Cecilia, we articulate crucial questions that we return to in the flow of our conversations: How might we encounter the Tomebamba as a complex body of water? What *gestures in proximity* might enable an encounter between our bodies and this complex body of water? What practices might make us receptive to the specificities of this encounter? In other words, pedagogically speaking, how might we attend and respond to "moments of contact in the present that open up to the unfolding and shifting reality of the things and lives we meet" (Todd, 2020, p. 1116)?

Inspired by these questions, Cecilia distances herself from teaching children about the Tomebamba (as in knowledge transmission and cognitive accumulation of facts) and from bringing out children's existing knowledge about the river (tapping into children's interests to make them visible). Instead, Cecilia carefully focuses on the *space of encounter* – the space children and the river co-inhabit and co-shape as they meet with each other. Inspired by the scholarship of Todd (2020), we suggest that these educational encounters are

> not merely spatially oriented, as meetings that occur in a physical context, but are also temporally marked. They are occurrences that transpire from one moment to the next in an arc of chronological time that opens up to both history's precedent and the future's probable and potential consequences as well as in a living time of sensory experiences in the present. (p. 1118)

Pedagogical engagements that attend to the encounter and thus decentre the solipsistic self (the child) are not easy in today's neoliberal educational contexts that privilege individualism. For Cecilia, focusing on encounters requires her to rethink her role as an educator by slowly moving from the peripheral role of facilitator or companion to joining the children in the fullness of their meetings with the Tomebamba – including the ruptures, vulnerabilities, and care that each encounter brings. Cecilia undoes the limits created for the teacher's role (be that traditional or progressive approaches). In the same way that the river's waters overflow when it rains, Cecilia overflows the limits of her teacher subjectivity. Outside these normative limits, she encounters the children differently.

Through paying attention to encounters with the Tomebamba, Cecilia and the children learn to notice its sensibilities, movements, and expressions. Yet, there is more than resonance here; there is also speculation. Trafí-Prats and Castro-Varela (2022) propose that "the focus of speculative inquiry is not on things or beings but on events that bring different entities together in a dynamic process of becoming in which something new is introduced in the world by a nexus of incidents that adhere to one another" (p. 5).

Watercolours resonate with the Tomebamba's waters; their movement and transparency propel children to explore the river's singularities in great detail and invent new relations through speculative imaginings. Textiles add yet another dimension, bringing the children to grapple with a river in constant flux. These encounters with watercolours and textiles give space to a distinctive emergent sensibility. Children are in an emergent relationship with the river. This shift in sensibility is important for education. As Todd (2003) proposes, it is sensibility that "grounds such selflessness not in some supreme effort of will but on the capacity to feel" (p. 52). Through watercolours and fast-moving textiles, the children "generate sensory experiences that become entangled in the emergence of who they are … in the present within an already existing relational world – a world that is composed not simply of solid objects [water], but of variation and flow" (Todd, 2020, p. 1123). Children in Puertas del Sol are immersed in an aesthetic encounter "to help them live and lead fulfilling lives in a context that is sensitive, attuned and responsive to" their interconnected and interdependent existence (p. 1111).

## Proximity Through Drawing

Drawing acts as a crucial element for children to create narratives that bring them into proximity with the river. For Cecilia, the act of drawing is reconfigured, from a tool for children to develop artistically toward a gesture that puts children in conversation with Tomebamba. Needless to mention, for Cecilia this shift was neither instant nor fully completed at an easily identifiable point in time. Rather, the reconfiguration demanded thoughtful critique of ideas that Cecilia (and other educators) lived with for a long time. Traditionally, drawing in early childhood is conceptualized, as Sunday, McClure, and Schulte (2014) explain, using "a modernist view of children's art as a romantic expression of inner emotional and/or developmental trajectories" (p. 1). This conception limits how drawing is introduced and employed in the classroom as well as its pedagogical possibilities. The challenge for Cecilia then involved both transgressing developmental norms and attending and attuning to a world beyond the individual child and toward the river and its inhabitants.

The work of atelierista Sylvia Kind has been an important inspiration for Cecilia, who thoughtfully puts into action Kind's rich descriptions of drawing:

> We entered together the gestural-heart-felt-bodied-experienced-rhythmic-movements of drawing and our perception of drawing becoming enlarged as we became more attuned to children's gestural and sonorous enactments and the rhythms and movements of drawing with others. There also is a need to keep in motion, especially if we think of drawing as a practice, never quite arriving, always moving towards a more attuned perception. (Kind, 2018, p. 10)

Taking these offerings seriously, Cecilia reimagines and reinvents herself as educator to consider children's drawings as social practices, as events, as modes of inquiry. In this process of reimagination and reinvention, Cecilia thinks with drawing, to notice the ways in which drawing lives and is lived among the children, how materials matter in the process of creating educational spaces, how children experiment with lives and worlds through drawing, how drawing propels children to imagine the otherwise as well as the possible/impossible, how drawing alters and repositions the river's relations, and how drawing sustains questions.

Drawing in Puertas del Sol becomes a mode of noticing Tomebamba and its relations, or, as Trafí-Prats and Castro-Varela (2022) write, a way "to widen the imagination around urban life beyond neoliberal and colonial subjectivities and geographies" (p. 1). Drawing serves as a way to sustain caring relations, as a way to carefully read the educational contexts in which children live, as a way to enable dialogue with children to collectively think about what kinds of questions and/or ideas they want to centre their attention on as the teacher continues nourishing the pedagogical propositions that might alter those very educational contexts. In the words of Trafí-Prats and Castro-Varela, drawing "could open the imagination for less passive ways of living with [the city] and appropriate them to develop other ways of making with them" (p. 1).

As with all modes of speculative curriculum making, Cecilia does not presume to know the entirety of what might be possible when she considers drawing beyond tradition. But it is the tentative and hopeful practices that propel Cecilia forward to collectively imagine many possibilities when she risks what is comfortable and known.

## Crafting Relations with the River

Conceptually, in Puertas del Sol we engage with what environmental humanities scholar Neimanis (2014) calls a "capacious aqueous reimagining" that challenges instrumentalized notions of water that treat it as "a resource for human flourishing" (p. 6). In Puertas del Sol, the river encounters "expand the imaginary of what water can be, of what water might need, and of our human responsibilities within a more-than-human aqueous ecology" (Neimanis, 2014, pp. 5–6). Challenging the notion of water as resource, Cecilia works with the idea of water as ecology – "that is, an ecology in which humans and other bodies of water (animal, vegetable, meteorological, geophysical) are always already implicated, as lively agents, in one another's well-being" (pp. 5–6).

The children, as they carefully work through/with Tomebamba's multiple relations, experience water in expansive, relational, and communally oriented ways. Unlike Western liberal individualist logics that introduce water as a right of humans and nonhuman life, Cecilia invites children to think of water "as an element to which we bear a far more complex relation, or even in which humans are not a central consideration" (Neimanis, 2014, p. 8). By presencing Tomebamba's waters and then reimagining them in the garden (using textiles and watercolours), Cecilia invites the children to think, to be, and to respond to "the liveliness and agency that animates [water] as a life – and yes, also death – force" (Neimanis, p. 10). In other words, Cecilia and the children "find ways of imagining watery nature as continuous with human nature, and therefore responsive to human actions, but in a way that does not deny waters their power and agency as collaborators" (p. 10). Rather than thinking of Tomebamba as a "strangely instrumentalized backdrop for our human dramas" (p. 10), Cecilia makes pedagogical decisions and offers curricular processes that build children's "sense of [their] shared presence and shared making of our hydrocommons" (p. 21).

Through this framing, careful acts of noticing the river's sensibilities, movements, and expressions displace the impoverished understandings of water/rivers often laid out in science education (Pacini-Ketchabaw & Clark, 2016). As Scherrer (2022) explains, "the removal of physical or emotive connection to place offers little to understand how to engage on relational terms and in some cases might offer haunted formations of placelessness or unknowing of place" (p. 196). As the documentation shows, Cecilia counters "the logics and coded knowledge within the curricular maps educators are contracted to work from" (Scherrer, p. 197). Instead, she *makes curriculum* that offers "alternative place-specific ways to see, engage with, and re-vision the world" (p. 197). This curriculum combines "moves to reclaim, reform, reconstitute" and even reinvent "other ways of knowing that are erased within siloed educational domains" (p. 196). In this garden, we reconstitute these other ways of knowing in the encounters with the river. We create pedagogies that emphasize thinking collectively following the logic of the river. We notice how our thoughts are also circular, how they have fluidity and movement. The children are engaged in "collective and kinful ways of living" (Scherrer, p. 199) with the Tomebamba, bringing pedagogical hope for livingness beyond impending extraction in Cuenca (see Juana Cordoba's exhibit: https://artishockrevista.com/2023/05/28/juana-cordova-no-todo-lo-que-brilla/).

## River's Own Relations

Approaching Tomebamba as expansive also entails engaging with the river's relationalities. Children notice that the river and rocks are in constant conversation, and they join this conversation by imagining how water leaves subtle traces on the river rocks. They dialogue about the clothes and plastic remnants that have now become another vital component of the river. They also imagine Tomebamba's shifting relations with weather systems and mountain ranges. And through these noticings, dialogues, and imaginings, children reinvent themselves as careful witnesses of complex and fluid relations.

As rocks take centre stage in drawings and dialogues, the children connect to important place relations. For centuries, rocks have held spiritual and cultural significance for Indigenous Andean peoples, who "revered certain boulders and outcroppings of rock, which they believed were animate and capable of interacting with human beings. Not only were certain stones sentient, but the Inka maintained that they possessed a sense of sight as well" (Dean, 2011, p. 152). As sentient and agentic, rocks would become fatigued, angry, sympathetic, or resistant; they could even suddenly weep "sanguineous tears" when they were moved from one location to another (Dean, 2019, p. 235). We do not suggest that we are attempting to recreate these ancient practices. Nevertheless, children in Puertas del Sol proceed to create memories that bring them closer to these ancient onto-epistemologies as they expand on current capitalist notions of ecology and justice that position nonhumans as resources available for extraction. Through drawing and speculative methods, the children imagine their bodies and lives in relation to the stones that nurture and are nurtured by Tomebamba's waters.

In Cuenca, as in other cities and towns in Ecuador, the river's stones continue to be important sites for Indigenous peasant women's labour, including washing clothes, cooking food, and grazing animals. Although governments increasingly restrict these practices (both by imposing regulatory policies and supporting extractivist projects and industrial capitalism that slowly poison local rivers (Trujillo et al., 2018), the majority of Cuencan children have witnessed these women's labour alongside Tomebamba, and very often the riverbanks are covered by a long spread of colourful clothing lying on the grass to be dried by the Andean sun. During their visits to the river, children become curious about how the river carries clothing that escapes during washing when the river is full, and how these wandering garments hug the rocks when the river is "thirsty." They also pay attention to the never-ending plastics deeply embedded in the banks and rocks of Tomebamba, which have changed the texture of the river in the past decades. To Cecilia these are noticings that cannot be pedagogically ignored. She invites the children to closely attend to what the river carries and leaves behind through the collective process of creating a blanket. Families join in, and after months of delicate work, children contemplate the huge blanket hugging the rocks left visible when the river is "sleepy." Weaving themselves into Tomebamba's memories, the children connect in relational ways to the river's complex watercourses.

Being in close relation with the Tomebamba involves fully attending to its movements and to the fact that the river is not always a harmonious body. Children encounter a flowing river with rushing waters and witness how it destroys everything in its path. The sound of a full and fast-moving Tomebamba brings the city to an edge, including children in Puertas del Sol. Cecilia embraces this "awakened" river, as the children call it. Inspired by the River Severn Estuary UK et al. (2021), we think of "rivers and floods" as "makers of life and landscapes" (p. 456).

So the children return to drawing and watercolours with questions such as: What might the flooding create? How might the floods change the city and us? What is life like with a flooding river? What does a "mighty" Tomebamba carry? How might the stones live with such a powerful river? The children are deeply affected by the "profound power of water(s) – differing waters – to shape the world very directly – physically, and all the cultural, ecological, and political diversity that does, and does not, gather around that" (River Severn Estuary UK et al., p. 456). For many months we attend to these river flows. They inspire us to consider also the temporal flows of our pedagogical work: the normative contractions and the dense modern inheritances that often prevent movement and inventive flux.

Puertas del Sol provided a glimpse of what is possible when capitalist and extractive logics are (momentarily) put on hold – or weakened – in an educational context to give space to logics of intimacy and care. In pandemic times, when life's precarity became starkly visible, in the itinerant school we proposed to attend to this precarity through pedagogies that brought children into proximity with the world, that is, into proximity with "a caring life force" (Carrière, 2023, p. 1) – the Tomebamba river. Rather than nurturing capitalist and extractivist processes that disconnect humans from the world, in Puertas del Sol we became closer to a river that is in ecological jeopardy. This approximation followed a relational, caring logic, yet one that did not ignore the complexities this river embodies in the twenty-first century. In our pedagogical work in this garden, the children and their teacher established multiple rhythms of a *corresponding proximity* with the river. Thus, our pedagogical interest was framed by an urge not to describe or define or explain but rather to stage small gestures articulated in correspondence, each following its own way yet dynamically going along *with* one another (Ingold, 2017).

As water has become "a particular site of resistance" in the work of Indigenous and non-Indigenous communities around the world (see World Water Walk 2024, n.d.), in Puertas del Sol we engaged pedagogically in "sustainable relations of care that posit the nonhuman and more-than-human not as passive entities reduced to use, consumption or domination but as entangled and agential" (Carrière, 2023, pp. 2–3). The hope is that these children will eventually be able to grapple with their deep interconnectivity and interdependency with water and, more specifically, with the rivers that sustain them.

# 11 Weaving into Existence: Stories and Correspondences in Las Cholas de Piedra Garden

WITH ALEX BERRY

Figure 11.1 Speculative Drawing: Las Cholas de Piedra Garden

In Las Cholas de Piedra garden, weaving with yarn initiates pedagogical processes that entangle children in the struggles posed by the garden's impermanence. An impermanence that is particularly striking for the children is the disappearance of the insects, spiders, and birds that once were present in the garden. Yarn, with its material force and lively memory, gathers children into collective questions and theories about what might be required for the creatures to return. At the same time, yarn knits the children into a complex Andean knowledge system that is spoken through acts of weaving. We, together with their educator, Carolina, engage with the pandemic's interruption of their school's familiar educational structure and its affectual dissonance by coming together around the potentiality of small daily acts of weaving with the children. As an act of life-making in the Andes (Arnold & Espejo, 2012), weaving together entwines us into pedagogical questions about how we might live well in the garden and what educational conditions might be required to begin sensing and responding to the absence of others with whom we share this place. In Las Cholas de Piedra garden, together we seek out new collective formations (Hamilton et al., 2021) for pandemic living by intentionally attuning to minor perceptual cues (Manning, 2016) proposed to us in weaving (https://viraltimes.climateactionchildhood.net/index.php/gardens/cholas-de-piedra-garden/).

In this chapter, we discuss how the bodied performance of Andean weaving – through its gestures, sequences, and improvisations – opens us up to a haptic sensitivity to the garden as a lively biocultural network that is actively made and remade (Arnold & Espejo, 2012), braided and rebraided. This impermanence requires consistent attention to our moving relations and dependencies with the garden and its multitudes of lifeforms. It is important to highlight that in initiating pedagogical processes specific to the Las Cholas de Piedra neighbourhood during a moment of uneven violence and deepened uncertainty in Ecuador (Altman & Valarezo, 2020), we do not seek to find *meaning* about the garden, or ourselves, through the act of weaving. Nor do we view the act of weaving with children as instilling a form of cultural resilience for overcoming adversity (Hamilton et al., 2021). Rather, we are interested in practices of weaving with children (Berry, 2022) and how Andean weaving techniques are concerned with how one lives in, and with, the world (Arnold & Espejo, 2012) in its impurity. Within the distinct pedagogical context of the itinerant school, where normative practices of schooling are no longer viable, weaving becomes a way of inventing a form of togetherness. Through our daily weavings, we create pedagogical processes that seek to activate a possible educational reality with children in the garden.

## Approximations, in the Midst of Yarn

As we've written elsewhere, weaving entwines into Cuenca's lively histories and material culture; at the same time, weaving transforms these conditions as we unevenly inherit them alongside children (Berry,

2022). Throughout the year at the itinerant school we collaborate with Carolina, the educator in Las Cholas de Piedra, to cultivate attention to weaving as a mode of thought and action. As the documentation shows, this attention enables weaving to become a material language in the garden, one which the children begin to think and speak. Weaving together opens up ways of coming to sense the garden in a manner distinct to the somatic properties of yarn and, later, a variety of Andean vegetable fibres.

The children first encounter the garden through yarn's abundant length. Bundles of yarn are unravelled and travel across the garden creating a marked distance between bodies. Yet, while yarn's undoings extend us across the wide spaces of the garden, its long lines materialize our entanglements with others, beyond our own will. These expansive visual coordinates proposed by yarn complicate notions of separation and control that had previously supposed our orientation to the garden as a space made safe for children during the pandemic. In the early days of the itinerant school project, educators attempt to strip the garden of its dogs, insects, materials, and proximities to others that were considered synonymous with risk. Yet yarn, through its ongoing loops and links, persistently tethers the children to the garden, to its inhabitants, and to each other. In the midst of yarn, children's extremities – legs, fingers, feet – become tied up with the extremities of others – prickles, stems, stumps. However hesitantly, these initial approximations to the garden are lived through the moving restrictions, uneasy gatherings, and generosities of yarn. Significantly, yarn confronts us with a recurring anxiety that is lived through the visibility of our proximities and possible contamination. As the educators reckon with stories of the virus travelling through the community and attempt to rationalize its unseen movements, yarn draws us together in ethical questions about how we might create pedagogies that simultaneously engage the children in these uncertainties, and how we might become answerable to the consequences of our differential participation in the virus's presence. Indeed, thinking through this participation demands attention to our collective obligation to the health of other humans. Yet, as many others have pointed out before us (e.g., Latour, 2020; van Dooren, 2020), becoming answerable to the pandemic's violence also requires that we devise new ways of living in good relation with animals, water, air, and earthly networks that maintain the healthy presence of pathogens across biomes (van Dooren, 2020). It is with these concerns at heart that we orient ourselves, with yarn, to Las Cholas de Piedra garden.

Carolina, responding to the instructive tensions proposed to us in meeting the garden through yarn's vitalities, enlaces yarn threads and vegetable fibres typically used in Andean weaving into daily curricular experiences with the children. Yarn, *cabuya* (a natural fibre), and *carrizo* (reeds) are carefully arranged in the garden each morning as materials to make our uneasy proximities to others felt and to mediate the children's thinking into the troubling absence of the garden's once-pesky insects, birds, and spiders. Simultaneously, Carolina shares with the children stories of knitting yarn with her grandmother along the stone-lined banks of Cuenca's Tomebamba river. Yarn has a close relationship with water and stones in the Andes, as weavers wind their threads around small river pebbles to hold their bundles between uses. The stone marks the heart of the bundle and ensures the yarn threads "run," echoing the ongoing flow of the river's waters (Arnold, 2018). In Ecuador, the arteries of sacred high-altitude rivers embroider the mountains like threads themselves; this relation between highland waters and thread figures a metaphor that is common across the Andes: "thread of life" (Vicuña, 1996). Yet, weaving in the Andes is much more than only metaphor. Weaving involves an active dialogue between humans and more-than-human others, where the movement of fibres and interlacing threads accompanies the unfolding formation of a broader biocultural space (Arnold, 2018). For Arnold (2018), weaving is the "ontological equivalent of rearing together mutually" (p. 2).

As part of what Arnold (2018) calls a *transformational ontology*, acts of weaving coordinate a continuity between the weaver, place, and their emerging coexistence (p. 8). In Las Cholas de Piedra garden, weaving is the mode through which we modestly begin to conceptualize this coexistence. Weaving together with the children enables us to transform the conditions of the garden as an educational space by nurturing the children's sensitivities to co-dependencies within the garden in ways that are specific to Andean weaving knowledges. Over time, the material processes of weaving create a circumstance for thinking with the garden as a place that is becoming in multiplicity, distinction, and, as a consequence, a proliferating divergence.

## Weaving Perception and Divergence in the Garden

Upon encountering scattered white feathers and traces of insects and spiders, the children speculate that the birds eat the insects and spiders and, after consumption, provide a home inside their stomachs where the insects and spiders continue to live. Other children argue that dogs eat the birds, insects, and spiders in shared moments at ground level. Engaging with these theories through acts of weaving, the children's deliberations begin to take shape in ways that are figured through the haptic rhythms of braiding, the affordances of certain materials, and the garden itself.

For instance, as seen in the documentation, as the children weave with thickly bundled cabuya from the Andean *Furcraea* leaf, Antonia's braid slowly takes circular form, spiralling round with a bowl-like resonance. She repeatedly layers fibre over fibre, consistently adjusting to meet the roundness of the braid. There is a rhythmic pattern worked through the hand as the growing coil of rolled cabuya proposes a motion that twists and runs in a wave-like tempo. This current flows from fibre to hand and back again, over and under, gradually echoing the half-moon figure of a bird's nest. As she weaves, Antonia suggests to the children that if the garden has nests, perhaps the birds will return along with the insects in their bellies. The children join Antonia in weaving nests and positioning them throughout the garden for the birds and insects: a gesture we view as a nonneutral invitation for a multispecies gathering.

At the same time, other children weave with fine synthetic yarn, using small looms they have made with sticks from the garden. Through the gesture of yarn's weft as it meets the warp of the loom, we attune to the material sensation of running thread and struggle to sustain its current with learning hands. When enlaced with yarn over time, the thin, star-like figure of the loom proposes a weave that the children suggest resembles a spider's web. The children experiment with the synchronicities of yarn and cabuya, rolled and tied carefully together in a series of rings that are hung like perches on the opportune folds of the trunks of Cycas trees. As shown in the documentation of Las Cholas de Piedra garden, both materials and the garden itself shape how the children's woven artifacts emerge and come to matter. For us, the processes and living artifacts of the children's weaving are pedagogically significant because they instigate an embodied form of attention to the distributed agency between children and the garden as they mutually create conditions for living together. Through the garden's nascent weaving pedagogies, we attempt to enlace the children into the connective web of life in the garden by centring this vital link between bodied gestures of weaving – the haptic, corporal, sensational essence of braiding – and their material effects.

Carolina continues to engage the children in these daily acts of weaving, and over several months, the garden becomes inundated with various nests and web-like structures that are woven as a gesture for the birds, insects, and spiders to return. Each "home" is made in response to the particularity of the creature who might inhabit it and as a consequence of the improvisational relationship between material and maker (Ingold, 2013; Kind, 2010; Pacini-Ketchabaw, Kind & Kocher, 2024) and the garden. The garden becomes crowded with a multiplicity of structures arranged above the ground, throughout the trees and bushes of the garden. The children propose that the garden has become a city; they grow even more perplexed by the expanding problem of what the city's growth might mean for the possibility of coexistence in the garden, where previously the presence of certain creatures had provoked the absence of others. Meeting this problem through the language of weaving, the children become knotted in discord amid an abundance of speculative theorizations and the impossible task of "managing" the city's complexity.

In response to these challenges, Carolina intensifies inconsistencies across the children's conversations and attempts to engage them in the distinctions that characterize both their collective inquiry and the garden itself. Inspired by what de la Cadena (2019) calls a "complex we," with the children, Carolina creates proximities to the garden and its multispecies community by carefully attending to "what each of us in the *we* are not" (p. 478, emphasis added). Within this conceptual frame, disparities among the children's theories are not comparative (Stengers, 2011), nor do they "cancel each other out" (de la Cadena, 2022, p. 446), but rather they become distinct through a "jointly inhabited relation" (p. 447). With Stengers (2011), we meet these distinctions as generative pedagogical potencies that activate divergent practices within the garden. Carolina intentionally arranges conditions for this divergence by bringing together a visual arrangement of the children's cut-out drawings, woven artifacts, structural prototypes, and her own notations and layering them over a large sketch of the garden's cityscape. She attempts to carefully and aesthetically sustain the singularity of each theory and artifact, creating an occasion for a democratic gathering that engages the children in the productive difficulties of being together within this multiplicity. Inviting the children to weave together, again, within this situation prepared by Carolina further activates weaving as a converging force that enables us to hold several ideas together and to think through their variance.

## Weaving as a Language of Life-Making in the Garden

*"To speak is to thread, and the thread weaves the world."*

Cecilia Vicuña, 1996

Across Ecuador, dialects of weaving are distinct to certain regions and their material and cultural specificities. In Ecuador's Andean mountains, the specific patterns and colours of woven objects figure a communicative structure that is shared across highland communities. As Vicuña writes, they thread and weave this world. These objects hold messages that are passed between people at various altitudes of the mountain. Yet, as Andean textual forms, woven artifacts do much more than only hold and transfer information (Arnold, 2023). Specific designs are instructive but not solely instrumental, as they speak in relation with dynamic cultural and ecological processes already alive in the world. In this sense, to weave is not only to create and share signification or meaning; weaving also shapes collective sensitivities and an ethos within a common ecocultural milieu (Arnold, 2023). In Las Cholas de Piedra garden, we view the children's woven nests and webs as small, living artifacts of participation toward the formation of such an ethos. Here, as with Álvarez (1987), to weave is to listen and speak within a complex knowledge system that shapes ways of perceiving, thinking, and acting within a community. The technical practice of weaving has to do with the vital process of *making* a life (Arnold, 2018; Cereceda, 1986), where woven artifacts and the materials used to create them are considered persons in their own right (Arnold, 2018). Each woven piece, or textile body, ensouls a material form that intimately links Andean social and biological lifeforms and landscapes (Arnold, 2018). In creating the pedagogical processes of Las Cholas de Piedra garden, we refer to Andean onto-epistemologies of textile weaving, whereby the weave is made through the openings and closings of the warp. Through the mouth of the warp, the weave comes to life as if it were eating and breathing (Arnold, 2018, p. 7). In the practice of these traditions, weavers create intimate material dialogues between animal and woven bodies by infusing the smells of lanolin and animal oils directly into the fibres of their weave.

As our pedagogical collaborations with Carolina move within/against prevailing educational paradigms, weaving together with children in Las Cholas de Piedra garden requires attention to what de la Cadena (2022) describes as "the metabolic need" of modern knowledge "to transform itself into what it cannot recognize" (p. 445). Thus, we acknowledge that Andean weaving knowledges perform beyond the "limits of what we can think" (p. 447). Taking seriously the incomprehensibility of Andean weaving cosmologies and resisting easy translations, we attempt to practice what Stengers (2008) has called a dissociation from capitalist impulse. In early childhood education, such an impulse might reduce weaving into recognizable terms, for instance, as an activity for children's entertainment, developmental gain, or even as a representation of the children's understanding of the garden. In our collaborations with Carolina, we are sensitive to how these individualist logics "rehearse a coloniality" (de la Cadena, 2022, p. 446) in the garden by overlooking the complex, "mutually reinforcing" dialogue between humans and others that is at the heart of Andean weaving arts (Arnold, 2018, p. 7). Las Cholas de Piedra's weaving pedagogies come into existence, in part, because of Carolina's temporary dissociation from these capitalist impulses in the itinerant school and the generative space this dissociation creates for her engagement with weaving – not as an activity for children to do but as a mode of thought and manner of being together with children and the garden. Considering children's woven structures as living beings is one of the shifts we take in reorienting to the garden's materiality and carefully figuring ourselves within its multispecies orchestra. Throughout the year, Carolina pays attention to the techniques and tact of certain weaving methods and the performance of materials as they structure the mannerisms and velocities of the children's collective braiding. Importantly, she attunes to the forms of togetherness that manifest through these practices.

As a modest (and imperfect) attempt at "making a life" together through the techniques of weaving (Arnold, 2018), the Las Cholas de Piedra weaving pedagogies crafted possibility for a manner of coexistence with the garden that was constituted by divergence and impermanence in a moving world. As the bricks-and-mortar school reopens following the itinerant school's academic year, the Las Cholas de Piedra pedagogies of weaving continue. The educators and children carry on weaving, both as a form of sense making that creates life and as a way of living. Yet, as we re-encounter our educational project within more traditional schooling parameters, capitalism's speed, duration, and compression has reached the teachers. Ecuador is now positioned in a state of increased social, ecological, and economic precarity amid exploitive international trade relations (Morán, 2021). Neoliberal pressures that existed before the pandemic refigure in novel forms. While the pandemic's pause afforded us an opening to experiment with weaving pedagogies for life making, neoliberalism now exerts an amplified force on the school to "catch up" on what was made temporarily absent. Without wanting to sound nostalgic, we are reminded that pedagogical openings need to be carefully nurtured, as they come with no guarantees.

# 12 Projected Into a Yet to Come: The Itinerant School and its Hauntology

This book tells a single story: what can happen when we think of an educational experience beyond conventional schooling models. We might say that the itinerant school has either brought education as we know it into a sharper focus or weakened its capitalist-driven focus. In either case, it might even be fair to conclude that the itinerant school has offered transformative educational experiences for the children, the educators, and us all. Yet, writing a conclusion summarizing what the itinerant school was and has accomplished (if anything) seems impossible to us. It is impossible because the itinerant school was not merely a physical space that delivered a conventional curriculum. For us, the itinerant school cannot be thought as an accomplishment or having a completion neatly pinned down in a conclusion. An excess pours out from the itinerant school, beautiful, vivid, and alive in our current work with Santana. It is palpable as we continue thinking within the multiple reverberations of the itinerant school or in the teachers' references to their experiences and in how it continues to generatively puncture their current daily practices. It is this excess that makes it difficult to write a conclusion.

If any provisional conclusion may be offered, it might best take the form of the question of whether the itinerant school has been an event. There is much that could be said about this question. For now, it will have to suffice to say that by "event" we are referring to that which happens as a supplement or as a rupture within the orders of a situation – such as in the domain of knowledge (schooling as we know it) – effecting thereby change or transformation. In other words, an event can be thought as an indeterminate radical difference on the basis of which one cannot carry on as before. We wonder if the itinerant school was an evental site because we have witnessed the *otherwise* it brought, and we still experience the indeterminacy it inaugurated and that prevents us from considering the experience of the itinerant school fully complete or concluded. It keeps our idea of school and schooling projected into a yet-to-come.

As we complete this book, two years after the time of the itinerant school, we experience a paradox or – to be more precise and to say it with Derrida – an *aporetic experience.* On one hand, we are confronted by the realization that the bonds and binds of conventional education (that is, schooling that focuses on progress and return) are not conducive of the thinking and practices generated in the itinerant school. When teachers and students returned to the material structure of the school, they usually returned also to familiar routines and curricular expectations. This return to formality speaks to the powerful disciplining force of institutionalized education, which can stifle the speculative, responsive, and situated pedagogies that the itinerant school so carefully fostered. The presence of physical walls, timetables, routines, and administrative normality reintroduced the very boundaries the itinerant school disrupted. On the other hand, there remains a constant spectral presence of the itinerant school. This presence might not be real enough to be visible as an "actual" or empirical transformation, but it is nonetheless able to profoundly haunt our current experiences and to work in uncanny possibilities that generatively disturb the daily practices of the teachers. It is often also evoked by the children who took part in the school. Because it is a spectral presence, its power might seem weak, but its haunting force is enough to keep a space of openings in multiple forms: in the form of questions (of "*what if*" and "*why*" and "*how this?*"), of reconfigurations (of power, and of possibility itself), and of otherwise doings. All these forms create openings for pedagogical gestures that evoke the itinerant school; at the same time, they also bring something yet unimagined and prompt us to inevitably ask: How is it that something past creates a future that haunts the present? This is a question of the event and a question of the itinerant school.

As we write these lines, we are immersed in the thickness of this aporetic experience. Although we might think that there was not enough faithfulness to the event of what the itinerant school could have been, we also often feel grateful for a school and for teachers' courage to embrace their hauntings and articulate pedagogical possibilities that follow from the event of this experience. These are practices that are not the automatic repetition of previous "know-hows" of supposed authorities. They are more of the order of a response; they create ethical bindings and relations of community within a collective search not bound up within the normative borders of an idea of schooling that we know perhaps too well. When these moments and practices occur, something other takes place in the order of schooling.

Thus, we are still engaged in this journey, still working to understand all that the itinerant school has been and is enabling, still engaged in conversations with the educators and families, and still revisiting the itinerant school documentation as we continue to collaborate with the school. This ongoing process reflects our commitment not to definitive answers or conclusions but to an open inquiry into what education has become and what it may yet be.

# References


Adams, G., Estrada-Villalta, S., Sullivan, D., & Markus, H. R. (2019). The psychology of neoliberalism and the neoliberalism of psychology. *Journal of Social Issues, 75*, 189–216. https://doi.org/10.1111/josi.12305

Altman, D., & Valarezo, J. C. (2020). Deaths and desperation mount in Ecuador, epicentre of coronavirus in Latin America. *The Conversation*. https://theconversation.com/deaths-and-desperation-mount-in-ecuador-epicenter-of-coronavirus-pandemic-in-latin-america-137015

Álvarez, S. G. (1987). Artesanías y tradición étnica en la Península de Santa Elena. *Artesanías de América, 25*, 45–119. Centro Interamericano de Artesanías y Artes Populares (CIDAP), Cuenca.

Anderson, B., & Harrison, P. (2016). The promise of non-representational theories. In B. Anderson & P. Harrison (Eds.), *Taking-place: Non-representational theories and geography* (pp. 1–34). Routledge.

Andrade, J. C. (1950). *La vasija de barro* [song]. www.facebook.com/watch/?v=1098671367412940

Arias, E. P. G. (2018). *La chakana del corazonar: Desde las espiritualidades y las sabidurías insurgentes de Abya Yala* [*The chakana of the heart: From the spiritualities and insurgent wisdoms of Abya Yala*]. Editorial Universitaria Abya-Yala.

Arnold, D. Y. (2018). Making textiles into persons: Gestural sequences and relationality in communities of weaving practice of the South Central Andes. *Journal of Material Culture, 23*(2), 239–60. https://doi.org/10.1177/1359183517750007

– (2019). The Andean material world. In L. J. Seligmann & K. S. Fine-Dare (Eds.), *The Andean world* (pp. 143–57). Routledge. https://doi.org/10.4324/9781315621715-10

– (2023). Weaving as writing: A serious omission in the Bolivian educational reform of 1994. *Cultura & Psyché, 4*, 47–65. https://doi.org/10.1007/s43638-023-00066-2

Arnold, D. Y., & Espejo, E. (2012). *Ciencia de tejer en los Andes: Estructuras y tecnicas de faz de urdimbre.* Instituta de Lengua y Cultura Aymara.

Baixauli Franco, M. Á. (Ed.). (2023). *Mundos por venir: Un punto de partida.* Colección Fuera de colección. Universitat Politècnica de València.

Barone Zallocco, O., & Díaz, S. R. (2021). Un (des)intento fugitivo de (a)bordar los (des)bordes. *Post(s), 7*(12), 28–51. http://dx.doi.org/10.18272/post(s).v7i7.2415

– (2023). Vitalidades pedagógicas: Sensibilidades y re-existencias en lo educativo. *Post(s), 9*(1), 12–23. https://doi.org/10.18272/post(s).v9i1.3149

Baudrillard, J. (1995). *Simulacra and simulation* (S. F. Glaser, Trans.). University of Michigan Press.

Beauclair, N. (2013). La reciprocidad andina como aporte a la ética occidental: Un ejercicio de filosofía intercultural. *Cuadernos Interculturales, 11*(21), 39–57. www.redalyc.org/articulo.oa?id=55229413003

Berardi, F. (2017). *Futurability: The age of impotence and the horizon of possibility.* Verso Books.

Berry, A. (2022). *Weaving child-plastic relations in the Ecuadorian Andes* [Doctoral dissertation, Western University]. Western University Electronic Thesis and Dissertation Repository. https://ir.lib.uwo.ca/etd/8475/

Berry, A., Vintimilla, C. D., & Pacini-Ketchabaw, V. (2020). Interrupting purity in Andean early childhood education: Documenting the impurities of a river. *Equity & Excellence in Education, 53*(3), 276–87. https://doi.org/10.1080/10665684.2020.1785974

Biesta, G. J. (2017). *Letting art teach: Art education after Joseph Beuys.* ArtEZ Press.

Biesta, G. J., & Osberg, D. (2007). Beyond re/presentation: A case for updating the epistemology of schooling. *Interchange, 38,* 15–29.

Bishop, C. (2006). *Participation.* Whitechapel.

– (2012). *Artificial hells: Participatory art and the politics of spectatorship.* Verso.

Blas, Z. (2012). Queer darkness. In C. Wiedemann & S. Zehle (Eds.), Depletion design: A glossary of network ecologies (pp. 127–32). Institute of Network Cultures. https://networkcultures.org/_uploads/tod/TOD%238_DEPLETION_DESIGN.pdf

Bombino, D. (2010). *Making learning visible: A Reggio-inspired project using pedagogical documentation.* Library and Archives Canada.

Bourriaud, N. (2002). *Relational aesthetics.* Les Presses du réel.

Braidotti, R. (2022). Critique, power, and the ethics of affirmation: Transformative ideals of justice in ethical and political thought. In T. Claviez & V. Marchi (Eds.), *Throwing the moral dice: Ethics and the problem of contingency* (pp. 145–61). Oxford University Press.

Carrière, M. (2023). Taking care of water: Katherena Vermette's river woman and Rita Wong's undercurrent. *Ariel, 54*(2), 1–24. https://doi.org/10.1353/ari.2023.0011

Cereceda, V. (1986). The semiology of Andean textiles: The talegas of Isluga. In J. V. Murra et al. (Eds.), *Anthropological history of Andean polities* (pp. 149–73). Cambridge University Press.

Climate Action Childhood Network. (2024). [Website]. https://climate actionchildhood.net/

Colebrook, C. (2002). The politics and potential of everyday life. *New Literary History, 33*(4), 687–706. https://doi.org/10.1353/nlh.2002.0036

Common Worlds Research Collective. (2020). Learning to become with the world: Education for future survival. UNESCO Futures of Education Report [Background paper]. https://unesdoc.unesco.org/ark:/48223 /pf0000374032

Cusicanqui, S. R. (2018). *Un mundo ch'ixi es posible: Ensayos desde un presente en crisis*. Tinta Limón.

de la Cadena, M. (2015). *Earth beings. Ecologies of practice across Andean worlds.* Duke University Press.

– (2019). An invitation to live together: Making the "complex we." *Environmental Humanities, 11*(2), 477–84.

– (2022). Stengers meets an Andean mountain that is not only such. In N. Bubandt & T. S. Wentzer (Eds.), *Philosophy on fieldwork: Case studies in anthropological analysis* (pp. 443–62). Routledge.

Dean, C. (2011). Rock sites/rock's sight: Reflections on site documentation. *Public Art Dialogue, 1*(2), 151–61. https://doi.org/10.1080/21502552.2011 .591540

– (2019). A rock and an art place: The Inkas' Collaconcho in context. *World Art, 9*(3), 231–58. https://doi.org/10.1080/21500894.2019.1601131

Despret, V. (2008). The becomings of subjectivity in animal worlds. *Subjectivity, 23*(1), 123–39. https://doi.org/10.1057/sub.2008.15

– (2015). Thinking like a rat. *Angelaki, 20*(2), 121–34. https://doi.org/10.1080 /0969725X.2015.1039849

– (2016). *What would animals say if we asked the right questions?* (B. Buchanan, Trans.) University of Minnesota Press, 2016. (Original work published 2012)

Deutsch Lynch, B. (2019). Water and power in the Peruvian Andes. In L. J. Seligmann & K. S. Fine-Dare (Eds.), *The Andean world* (pp. 44–63). Routledge.

di Paoloantonio, M. (2023). *Education and democracy at the end: The crisis of sense.* Springer Nature.

Duschatzky, S. (2005). Hilos artesanales de composición social. Notas sobre experiencias juveniles en la escuela. *Nómadas, 23*, 76–84.

– (2016). Merodeos en torno de la transmisión. *Voces de la educación, 1*(2), 23–6.

Duschatzky, S., & Aguirre, E. (2019). *Des-armando escuelas*. Noveduc Libros.

Eco, U. (1989). The poetics of the open work. In *The open work* (A. Cancogni, Trans.), 251. Harvard University Press. (Original work published 1962)

Edwards, C., Gandini, L., & Forman, G. (Eds.). (2011). *The hundred languages of children: The Reggio Emilia experience in transformation*. Bloomsbury USA.

Erikson, C. L. (2019). The domesticated landscapes of the Andes. In L. J. Seligmann & K. S. Fine-Dare (Eds.), *The Andean world* (pp. 29–44). Routledge.

Esposito, R. (2021). Vitam instituere. In F. Castrillón & T. Marchevsky (Eds.), *Coronavirus, psychoanalysis, and philosophy: Conversations on pandemics, politics and society* (pp. 87–8). Routledge.

Gatt, C., & Ingold, T. (2020). From description to correspondence: Anthropology in real time. In W. Gunn, T. Otto, & R. C. Smith (Eds.), *Design anthropology: Theory and practice* (pp. 139–58). Routledge.

Giamminuti, S. (2009). *Pedagogical documentation in the Reggio Emilia education project: Values, quality, and community in early childhood settings* (Doctoral dissertation, University of Western Australia).

Gibson-Graham, J. K., Cameron, J., & Healy, S. (2016). Commoning as a postcapitalist politics. In A. Amin & P. Howell (Eds.), *Releasing the commons: Rethinking the future of the commons* (pp. 192–212). Routledge.

Glissant, É. (1997). *Poetics of relation*. University of Michigan Press.

Glockner, V., Borzacchiello, E., Torres, R. M., Faria, C., Danze, A., Herrera-Martínez, E., Garcia, G. & Niño-Vega, N. (2023). The cuerpo-territorio of displacement: A decolonial feminist geopolitics of re-existencia. *Geopolitics*, 1–25. https://doi.org/10.1080/14650045.2023.2213639

Gose, P. (2019). The Andean circulatory cosmos. In L. J. Seligmann & K. S. Fine-Dare (Eds.), *The Andean world* (pp. 115–28). Routledge. https://doi.org/10.4324/9781315621715-8

Griffin, S. (1995). *The eros of everyday life: Essays on ecology, gender, and society*. Doubleday.

Hamilton, J. M., Zettel, T., & Neimanis, A. (2021). Feminist infrastructure for better weathering. *Australian Feminist Studies, 36(109)*, 237–59.

Haraway, D. J. (1991). *Simians, cyborgs, and women: The reinvention of nature*. Routledge.

– (2005). The biopolitics of postmodern bodies: Constitutions of self in immune system discourse. In M. Fraser & M. Greco (Eds.), *The body: A reader* (pp. 242–6). Routledge.

– (2008). *When species meet*. University of Minnesota Press.

– (2016). *Staying with the trouble: Making kin in the Chthulucene*. Duke University Press.

Hathaway, M. (2015). Wild elephants as actors in the Anthropocene. In Human Animal Research Network (Ed.), *Animals in the Anthropocene: Critical perspectives on non-human futures* (pp. 221–42). Sydney University Press.

Ingala, E. (2023). Líneas invisibles que hacen y deshacen: Sobre la potencia del umbral. In M. Á. Baixauli Franco (Ed.), *Mundos por venir: Un punto de partida* (pp. 59–70). Colección Fuera de colección. Universitat Politècnica de València.

Ingold, T. (2011). *Being alive: Essays on movement, knowledge and description.* Routledge.

– (2013). *Making: Anthropology, archaeology, art, and architecture.* Routledge.

– (2017). On human correspondence. *The Journal of the Royal Anthropological Institute, 23*(1), 9–27. https://doi.org/10.1111/1467-9655.12541

– (2022a). On not knowing and paying attention: How to walk in a possible world. *Irish Journal of Sociology, 31*(1). https://doi.org/10.1177/07916035221088546

– (2022b). When ant meets spider: Social theory for arthropods. In *Being alive: Essays on movement, knowledge, and description.* Routledge.

– (2023). On not knowing and paying attention: How to walk in a possible world. *Irish Journal of Sociology, 31*(1), 20–36.

Jardine, D. (2008). On the while of things. *Journal of the American Association for the Advancement of Curriculum Studies,* 4. https://ojs.library.ubc.ca/index.php/jaaacs/article/view/187670/185769

Kind, S. (2010). Art encounters: Movements in the visual arts and early childhood education. In V. Pacini- Ketchabaw (Ed.), *Flows, rhythms, & intensities of early childhood education curriculum* (pp. 113–31). Peter Lang.

– (2018). Collective improvisations: The emergence of the early childhood studio as an event-full place. In C. M. Schulte & C. M. Thompson (Eds.), *Communities of practice: Art, play, and aesthetics in early childhood* (pp. 5–21). Springer.

Klaus, H. D. (2019). Life and death in the central Andes: Human biology, violence, and burial patterns in ancient Peru. In L. J. Seligmann & K. S. Fine-Dare (Eds.), *The Andean world* (pp. 96–111). Routledge. https://doi.org/10.4324/9781315621715-7

Krechevsky, M., Mardell, B., Rivard, M., & Wilson, D. (2013). *Visible learners: Promoting Reggio-inspired approaches in all schools.* John Wiley & Sons.

Lakoff, G., & Johnson, M. (2003). *Metaphors we live by.* The University of Chicago Press. (Original work published 1980)

Latour, B. (1993). *We have never been modern.* Harvard University Press.

– (2020). Where to land after the pandemic (S. Muecke, Trans.). www.bruno-latour.fr/node/852.html

Leggo, C. (2005). The heart of pedagogy: On poetic knowing and living. *Teachers and Teaching: Theory and Practice, 11*(5), 439–55.

Libertson, J. (2012). *Proximity: Levinas, Blanchot, Bataille, and communication.* Springer Science & Business Media.

MacLeod, J., & Neimanis, A. (2013). *Thinking with water.* McGill-Queen's University Press.

Manning E. (2008). Coloring the virtual. *Configurations, 16*(3), 325–46. https://doi.org/10.1353/con.0.0063

– (2013). The dance of attention. *Inflexions, 6,* 337–64. http://inflexions.org/n6_manning.html

– (2016). *The minor gesture.* Duke University Press.

– (2020). Radical pedagogies and metamodelings of knowledge in the making. *Critical Studies in Teaching and Learning (CriSTaL), 8*(SI), 1–16. https://doi.org/10.14426/cristal.v8iSI.261

Manning, E., & Massumi, B. (2014). *Thought in the act: Passages in the ecology of experience.* University of Minnesota Press.

McKittrick, K. (Ed.). (2015). *Sylvia Wynter: On being human as praxis.* Duke University Press.

McNulty, M. M. (2019). Speculative fiction, post human desire, and inquiry of currere. *Journal of Curriculum Theorizing, 34*(5), 75–85. https://journal.jctonline.org/index.php/jct/article/view/875

Morán, S. (2021, January). The U.S. sends more than 100 containers per month with its plastic waste to Ecuador. *Plan V.* www.planv.com.ec/us-sends-more-100-containers- month-its-plastic-waste-ecuador

Mustola, M. (2019). Why is a live chicken banned from the kindergarten? Two lessons learned from teaching posthuman pedagogy to university students. *Educational Philosophy and Theory, 51*(14), 1434–43. https://doi.org/10.1080/00131857.2018.1553712

Nancy, J. L. (2000). *Being singular plural.* Stanford University Press.

– (2021). A much too human virus. In F. Castrillón & T. Marchevsky (Eds.), *Coronavirus, psychoanalysis, and philosophy: Conversations on pandemics, politics and society* (pp. 63–5). Routledge.

Neimanis, A. (2014). Alongside the right to water, a posthumanist feminist imaginary. *Journal of Human Rights and the Environment, 5*(1), 5–24. http://dx.doi.org/10.4337/jhre.2014.01.01

Neimanis, A., & McLauchlan, L. (2022). Composting (in) the gender studies classroom: Growing feminisms for climate changing pedagogies. *Curriculum Inquiry, 52*(2), 218–34. https://doi.org/10.1080/03626784.2022.2041982

Nxumalo, F., Vintimilla, C. D, & Nelson, N. (2018). Pedagogical gatherings in early childhood education: Mapping interferences in emergent curriculum. *Curriculum Inquiry, 48*(4), 433–53. https://doi.org/10.1080/03626784.2018.1522930

Pacini-Ketchabaw, V., & Clark, V. (2016). Following watery relations in early childhood pedagogies. *Journal of Early Childhood Research, 14*(1), 98–111. https://doi.org/10.1177/1476718X14529281

– 2024. *Encounters with materials in early childhood education* (2nd ed.). Routledge.

Pacini-Ketchabaw, V., Vintimilla, C. D., Berry, A., Frankowski, A., & de Castro, A. (2020). Plastic childhoods: Noticing toxic intra-dependencies in Andean early childhood [Website]. https://riverplasticities.climateactionchildhood.net/

Peters, M. A., & Humes, W. (2003). Education in the knowledge economy [Editorial]. *Policy Futures in Education, 1*(1). https://doi.org/10.2304%2Fpfie.2003.1.1.1

Phelan, A. M., & Rüsselbæk Hansen, D. (2021). Toward a "thoughtful lightness": Education in viral times. *Prospects, 51*(1), 15–27.

Potts, A. (2012). *Chicken*. Reaktion Books.

Potts, A., & Haraway, D. (2010). Kiwi chicken advocate talks with California dog companion. *Feminism & Psychology, 20*(3), 318. https://doi.org/10.1177/0959353510368118

Price, E. K., & van Eeden-Wharton, A. (2023). Spiderly sympoiesis: Tensegral tentacularity and speculative clews. *Qualitative Inquiry, 29*(1), 179–99. https://doi.org/10.1177/10778004221099566

Puig de la Bellacasa, M. (2015). Making time for soil: Technoscientific futurity pace of care. *Social Studies of Science, 45*(5), 691–716. https://doi.org/10.1177/0306312715599851

– (2017). *Matters of care: Speculative ethics in more than human worlds*. University of Minnesota Press.

– (2019). Re-animating soils: Transforming human-soil affections through science, culture, and community. *The Sociological Review, 67*(2), 391–407. https://doi.org/10.1177/0038026119830601

Purewal, R., Christley, R., Kordas, K., Joinson, C., Meints, K., Gee, N., & Westgarth, C. (2017). Companion animals and child/adolescent development: A systematic review of the evidence. *International Journal of Environmental Research and Public Health, 14*(3), 234. www.ncbi.nlm.nih.gov/pmc/articles/PMC5369070/

Rinaldi, C. (2021). *In dialogue with Reggio Emilia: Listening, researching and learning* (2nd ed.). Routledge.

The River Severn Estuary UKBahíaAdair, Sonora, Mexico, Jones, O., & Green, H. (2022). Rivers – mouths – tides – memories: A creative, inter-deep-mapping of two river/tidal places. Love of place, memory and affect; movements, patterns, marks, and practices of care. *River Research and Applications, 38*(3), 453–69. https://doi.org/10.1002/rra.3887

Roberts-Holmes, G., & Moss, P. (2021). *Neoliberalism and early childhood education: Markets, imaginaries, and governance*. Routledge.

Rose, D. B., & van Dooren, T. (2021). Animist lures: Arts of witness. In J. M. Hamilton, S. Reid, P. van Gelder, & A. Neimanis (Eds.), *Feminist, queer, anticolonial propositions for hacking the Anthropocene: Archive* (pp. 32–7). Open Humanities Press. www.openhumanitiespress.org/books/titles/feminist-queer-anticolonial-propositions-for-hacking-the-anthropocene/

Roy, A. (2020, April 3). The pandemic is a portal. *Financial Times*. www.ft.com/content/10d8f5e8-74eb-11ea-95fe-fcd274e920ca

Sammells, C. A. (2019). Production, trade, reciprocity, and markets. In L. J. Seligmann & K. S. Fine-Dare (Eds.), *The Andean world* (pp. 251–65). Routledge. https://doi.org/10.4324/9781315621715-17

Scherrer, B. D. (2022). "Like you can tell a river where to go": Floods, ecological formations, and storied pedagogies of place. *Curriculum Inquiry*, 52(2), 187–204. https://doi.org/10.1080/03626784.2022.2041977

Snaza, N. (2019). *Animate literacies: Literature, affect, and the politics of humanism*. Duke University Press.

– (2021). Vagueness and care: On affect and literacy. *Reading Research Quarterly*, *56*(2), 253–6. https://doi.org/10.1002/rrq.364

Stengers, I. (2005). Introductory notes on an ecology of practices. *Cultural Studies Review*, *11*(1), 183–96.

– (2008). Experimenting with refrains: Subjectivity and the challenge of escaping modern dualism. *Subjectivity*, *22*(1), 38–59. https://doi.org/10.1057/sub.2008.6

– (2011). Comparison as a matter of concern. *Common Knowledge*, *17*(1), 48–63.

– (2015). *In catastrophic times: Resisting the coming barbarism* (A. Goffey, Trans.). Open Humanities Press.

– (2017). The insistence of possibles: Towards a speculative pragmatism. *Parse*, *7* (Autumn), 12–19. https://parsejournal.com/article/the-insistence-of-possibles%E2%80%A8-towards-a-speculative-pragmatism/

Stengers, I., & Debaise, D. (2017). The insistence of possibles: Towards a speculative ragmatism. *Parse Journal*, *7*, 13–19.

Sunday, K., McClure, M., & Schulte, C. (2014, May). Introduction: Art & early childhood – Personal narratives and social practices. *Bank Street Occasional Paper Series*, *2014*(31). https://doi.org/10.58295/2375-3668.1022

Taylor, A. (2013). *Reconfiguring the natures of childhood*. Routledge.

Taylor, A., & Pacini-Ketchabaw, V. (2017). Kids, raccoons, and roos: Awkward encounters and mixed affects. *Children's Geographies*, *15*(2), 131–45. https://doi.org/10.1080/14733285.2016.1199849

– (2018). *The common worlds of children and animals: Relational ethics for entangled lives*. Routledge.

Timeto, F. (2021). Becoming-with in a compost society: Haraway beyond posthumanism. *International Journal of Sociology and Social Policy*, *41*(3/4), 315–30. https://doi.org/10.1108/IJSSP-08-2019-0158

Todd, S. (2001). "Bringing more than I contain": Ethics, curriculum, and the pedagogical demand for altered egos. *Journal of Curriculum Studies*, *33*(4), 431–50. https://doi.org/10.1080/002202701300200911

– (2003). *Learning from the other: Levinas, psychoanalysis, and ethical possibilities in education*. SUNY Press.
– (2015). Experiencing change, encountering the unknown: An education in "negative capability" in light of Buddhism and Levinas. *Journal of Philosophy of Education, 49*(2), 240–54. https://doi.org/10.1111/1467-9752.12139
– (2020). Creating aesthetic encounters of the world, or teaching in the presence of climate sorrow. *Journal of Philosophy of Education, 54*(4), 1110–25. https://doi.org/10.1111/1467-9752.12478
– (2023). Expanding the publicness of education: Worlding the world in a time of climate emergency. In C. A. Säfström & G. Biesta (Eds.), *The new publicness of education: Democratic possibilities after the critique of neo-liberalism* (ch. 12). Routledge.
Trafí-Prats, L., & Castro-Varela, A. (2022). Visual participatory arts based research in the city. In L. Trafí-Prats & A. Castro-Varela (Eds.), *Visual participatory arts based research in the city: Ontology, aesthetics, and ethics* (pp. 1–19). Routledge.
Trujillo, C. A., Rangel, J. A. M., Carrera, J. R. A., & Tapia, K. R. L. (2018). Meanings of water for the Fakcha Llakta Indigenous community of Otavalo, Ecuador. *Ambiente & Sociedade, 21*. https://doi.org/10.1590/1809-4422asoc0100r3vu18l1ao
Tsing, A. (2020). When the things we study respond to each other. In A. Jaque, M. O. Verzier, & L. Pietroiusti (Eds.), *More-than-human* (pp. 16–27). Het Nieuwe Instituut.
Tuck, E., & Yang, K. W. (2012). Decolonization is not a metaphor. *Decolonization: Indigeneity, Education & Society 1*(1): 1–40. https://jps.library.utoronto.ca/index.php/des/article/view/18630
van Dooren, T. (2019). *The wake of crows: Living and dying in shared worlds*. Columbia University Press. https://doi.org/10.7312/van-18282
– (2020). Pangolins and pandemics: The real source of this crisis is human, not animal. *New Matilda*. https://newmatilda.com/2020/03/22/pangolins-and-pandemics-the-real-source-of-this-crisis-is-human-not-animal/
van Manen, M. (1990). *Researching lived experience: Human science for an action sensitive pedagogy*. SUNY Press.
Vecchi, V. (2002). *Art and creativity in Reggio Emilia: Exploring the role and potential of ateliers in early childhood education*. Routledge.
Vicuña, C. (1996). *Palabra e hilo*. Morning Star Publications.
Vintimilla, C. D. (2020). Relational openings for the otherwise: Thinking community as what is not. In W. O. Kohan & B. Weber (Eds.), *Thinking, childhood, and time: Contemporary perspectives on the politics of education* (ch. 11). Lexington Books.
– (2023). Critique, estrangement, and speculative envisioning: Pedagogical thinking and otherwise educational worlds. *Philosophical Inquiry in Education, 30*(1), 16–25.

Vintimilla, C. D., & Berger, I. (2019). Colaboring: Within collaboration's degenerative processes. In B. D. Hodgins (Ed.), *Feminist research for 21st-century childhoods: Common worlds methods* (pp. 187–96). Bloomsbury Academic.

Vintimilla, C. D., & Kind, S. (2021). Choreographies of practice: Mutualities and sympoetic becomings in early childhood teacher education. In H. Park & C. Schulte (Eds.), *Visual arts with young children: Practices, pedagogies, and learning* (pp. 33–46). Routledge. https://doi.org/10.4324/9781003020776

Vintimilla, C. D., & Pacini-Ketchabaw, V. (2020). Weaving pedagogy in early childhood education: on openings and their foreclosure. *European Early Childhood Education Research Journal, 28*(5), 628–41. https://doi.org/10.1080/1350293X.2020.1817235

Walcott, R. (2021). *The long emancipation: Moving toward Black freedom*. Duke University Press.

Walcott, R., & Abdillahi, I. (2019). *Blacklife: Post-BLM and the struggle for freedom*. ARP Books.

Wien, C. A. (2013). *Making learning visible through pedagogical documentation*. Queen's Printer for Ontario.

Wolff, L.-A., Vuorenpää, S., & Sjöblom, P. (2018). Chicken raising in a diverse Finnish classroom: Multidimensional sustainability learning. *Sustainability, 10*(11), 3886. https://doi.org/10.3390/su10113886

World Water Walk 2024. (n.d.). Walk a little in spirit with those that walk a lot. www.worldwaterwalk.org/

Zaragocin, S., & Caretta, M. A. (2020). *Cuerpo-territorio*: A decolonial feminist geographical method for the study of embodiment. *Annals of the American Association of Geographers, 111*(5), 1503–18. https://doi.org/10.1080/24694452.2020.1812370

# Index